How
Scripts
Are
Made

Inga Karetnikova

Southern Illinois University Press
Carbondale and Edwardsville

Copyright © 1990 by the Board of Trustees, Southern Illinois University
All rights reserved
Printed in the United States of America
Edited by Kathryn Koldehoff
Production & design by Linda Jorgensen-Buhman

93   92   91   90   4   3   2   1

Library of Congress Cataloging-in-Publication Data

Karetnikova, Inga.
  How scripts are made   /   Inga Karetnikova.
     p.   cm.
  Includes bibliographical references.
  1. Motion picture authorship.   2. Motion picture plays—Technique.
I. Title.
PN1996.K24   1990
808.2'3—dc20   89-26186
ISBN 0-8093-1379-0   CIP
ISBN 0-8093-1380-4 (pbk.)

The paper used in this publication meets the minimum requirements of
American National Standard for Information Sciences—Permanence of
Paper for Printed Library Materials, ANSI Z39.48-1984. ∞

To Paul and Anne

Contents

Introduction

More than half a century ago Fritz Lang, the renowned German director, compared the making of a film with the building of a medieval cathedral, a comparison that has been reiterated often. Indeed, a film is created by a great number of experts, just as architects, masons, engineers, sculptors, painters, and many others took part in the creation of a cathedral.

One of the main roles in the "building" of a film belongs to the screenwriter, who is the first to visualize the future film and who draws up its "blueprint"—the *screenplay* or, as it is often referred to, the *script*. When written by a master, it can fascinate the reader in the same way that any good piece of writing can. But unlike that of a novel or of a short story, which is a finished product, the ultimate goal of a screenplay is to become a film.

The screenplay has a certain format that is observed by every screenwriter, from beginners to professionals. Everything in it—the title of the scene, the description of the action, the dialogue—has its designated place. Some details of the screenplay format have changed over time. For example, in the past it was considered necessary to number each scene. As the screenplay has become a more readable literary form, today the scene numbers are omitted. Recently, there have also been some changes in the page design (the width of the lines and the spacing between them), but there is always an established, current format that the screenwriter must know and obey.

It is not difficult to learn the format or even to master the style of scene description—to write clearly in short, concise phrases, describing only the action and the setting. The difficulty is developing a screen story populated by believable characters, creating an expressive and logical relationship between the scenes by manipulating screen space and screen time, knowing what to omit from the story and what to emphasize, and finally, writing dialogue that sounds real but that does not simply copy everyday speech. Mastering all of these skills is a challenge, and precisely this mastery, along with the ability to see each scene while writing it, is the essence of the screenwriter's craft.

There are no established academic methods for teaching this craft (as, for example, there are no set ways of teaching how to write poetry or novels). The traditional method for teaching art may be helpful. Since ancient times, this method has been based on the detailed study of great works and the scrupulous analysis of them. Only after having passed through this training could the pupil create a masterpiece (as it was called in medieval workshops) and become a professional. The different works and styles that were studied by the pupil provided the foundation for mastery.

Students often repeat the misleading opinion that art is learned from life. Of course, everyday life is their material—boundlessly rich and always fascinating, a source of observation, thought, and knowledge— but they learn art from a different source. Early in the twentieth century, the celebrated French painter Pierre Renoir (father of the no less celebrated film director Jean Renoir) advised young painters to learn their craft not on the street but in the museum. Screenwriters, in their way, should do the same—learn their craft from the masters.

How Scripts Are Made is an analysis of eight classic screenplays, and one novel written in cinematic style, which may serve as models in the study of screenwriting. Each chapter in the book, except the last, is devoted to one script. Using each script as an example, various aspects of screenwriting are discussed and analyzed. How scripts are written and what makes them work is my focus; I do not present cultural or scholarly examinations of them. Only chapter 1 contains a short historical survey of the development of the screenplay.

How Scripts Are Made is designed to take the film student through one semester of classroom or independent study. While studying the book, reading the suggested scripts, and viewing the films based on them, the student should develop an original project: a screenplay for a short or, in some cases, a full-length dramatic film. Examination of the scripts included will provide both the teacher and the students with points of reference for problem solving in the students' original projects. And the sequence of the chapters will help the student to proceed from general problems of screenwriting, such as structuring techniques (chapter 2), to more specific ones, such as mastering suspense (chapter 5) or developing the symbolic meaning of details (chapter 7).

The order in which the book is studied can be altered slightly to fit the teacher's schedule; for instance, chapter 3 can be discussed after chapter 4, but the general order of the chapters should be followed. Chapter 8, for example, should be discussed at the end of the course when the student will be sufficiently prepared to tackle the task of writing screen dialogue.

Chapter 9, the last in the book, differs from the others in that it discusses a novel rather than a screenplay. But the purely cinematic style of the novel turns it into a helpful tool in teaching screenwriting.

A series of exercises for each chapter, dealing with the style of scene description, with screen characters, dialogue, and so forth, is presented in appendix A. All of these exercises have been used successfully by the students in my own screenwriting classes.

How Scripts Are Made can be useful not only to novice screenwriters but to students of film in general. The knowledge of how scripts are made is necessary for both future film directors and film scholars.

Several people contributed to the creation of this book. I thank Peggy Troupin, Chris Santos, and Veronica Beaulieu for their assistance. I also thank Southern Illinois University Press's James D. Simmons for his patience and Kathryn Koldehoff for her editing.

How Scripts Are Made

1.
The Beginning of Screenwriting

Nosferatu, a Symphony of Horror
by Henrik Galeen

Nosferatu, a Symphony of Horror, 1922
Director: Friedrich Murnau
Script: Henrik Galeen

Friedrich Murnau (1888–1931), one of the best and most innovative German directors of the silent era, studied art, literature, and philosophy in Heidelberg before he settled in Berlin. There he worked for the great stage director Max Reinhardt as an actor and occasionally as his assistant. During World War I, Murnau compiled propaganda films for the government, and when the war ended, he worked in the famous government-subsidized studios — Universum Film Aktiengesellschaft (UFA). It is unfortunate that Murnau's earliest films have been lost, all of them scripted by some of the most talented writers of the German cinema's "Golden Age."

It was with *Nosferatu* that Murnau first gained recognition in 1922. The film spawned the myriad remakes and variations of the Dracula story that have appeared ever since its release; yet Murnau's is still the quintessential version, with its poetic visual language and distinctive personal style both expressionistic and almost documentary. Most of the film — the landscapes, the main character's home town, the castle—was shot on location. Murnau knew how to invest the familiar with a sense of horror.

In 1924, *The Last Laugh,* with its subjective camera viewpoint, brought Murnau international success and an attractive offer to work for Fox Studios in Hollywood. His first American film, *Sunrise,* was a perfect blend of American optimism and German darkness.

Murnau formed an unlikely partnership with the legendary documentarist Robert Flaherty in 1929. The only film that they produced, *Tabu,* was shot on location in the South Seas. In 1931, a week before the premiere of the film, Murnau died in an automobile crash in California.

The scenario for *Nosferatu* was adapted from Bram Stoker's novel *Dracula* by Henrik Galeen (1882–1949), an actor and director, who was also one of the most important screenwriters working in Germany in the 1920s. He had an instinct for cinema and wrote his scripts with the camera in mind. Among his best works, besides *Nosferatu,* are *The Student of Prague* (1926) and *After the Verdict* (1928), which he both directed and scripted.

Murnau was fond of the *Nosferatu* script. Some pages of the original have the director's sketches on the back and the subtitles suggested by him.

Galeen imigrated to the United States after Hitler came to power, yet unlike many of his compatriots, he never established a career in Hollywood and faded into obscurity.

The first scripts looked much like shopping lists: they enumerated the objects and the scenes to be shot, and nothing in them suggested a readable text. This was true even for the script of the popular *A Trip to the Moon* (1902), written by its director and producer George Méliès, a great French showman, inventor, magician, and filmmaker. The entire script of this fourteen-minute movie follows:

1. The scientific congress at the Astronomic Club.
2. Planning the trip. Appointing the explorers and servants. Farewell.
3. The workshops. Constructing the projectile.
4. The foundries. The chimney-stacks. The casting of the monster gun.
5. The astronomers enter the shell.
6. Loading the gun.

7. The monster gun. March past the gunners. Fire!!! Saluting the flag.
8. The flight through space. Approaching the moon.
9. Landing right in the eye!!!
10. Flight of the shell into the moon. Appearance of the earth from the moon.
11. The plain of craters. Volcanic eruption.
12. The dream (the Solies, the Great Bear, Phoebus, the Twin Sisters, Saturna).
13. The snowstorm.
14. 40 degrees below zero. Descending a lunar crater.
15. Into the interior of the moon. The giant mushroom grotto.
16. Encounter with the Selenites. Homeric flight.
17. Prisoners!!!
18. The kingdom of the moon. The Selenite army.
19. The flight.
20. Wild pursuit.
21. The astronomers find the shell again. Departure from the moon.
22. Vertical drop into space.
23. Splashing into the open sea.
24. At the bottom of the ocean.
25. The rescue. Return to port.
26. The great fete. Triumphal march past.
27. Crowning and decorating the heroes of the trip.
28. Procession of Marines and the Fire Brigade.
29. Inauguration of the commemorative statue by the manager and the council.
30. Public rejoicings.[1]

Only if one is familiar with Méliès's imaginative and funny movie can one connect this "list" to the visual images and recognize some of the scenes described by just one or two words ("17. Prisoners!!!"; "20. Wild pursuit"). Méliès did not provide specifics about characters or scenery, and his sketchy lines do not constitute a coherent continuity of action. And yet this early, rudimentary manifestation of screenwriting is a concise presentation of scenes to be filmed and their proper chronological order.

A script that was written only one year later by the famous American director Edwin S. Porter for *The Great Train Robbery* (1903) is much more advanced and gives the reader a distinct image of the film.

Scene 1:   *Interior of railroad telegraph office.* Two masked robbers enter and compel the operator to get the "signal
block" to stop the approaching train, and make him
write a fictitious order to the engineer to take water at
this station, instead of "Red Lodge," the regular water-
ing stop. The train comes to a standstill (seen through
window of office); the conductor comes to the window,
and the frightened operator delivers the order while the
bandits crouch out of sight, at the same time keeping
him covered with their revolvers. As soon as the conductor leaves, they fall upon the operator, bind and gag
him, and hastily depart to catch the moving train.

Scene 2:   *Railroad water tower.* The bandits are hiding behind the
tank as the train, under the false order, stops to take water. Just before she pulls out they stealthily board the
train between the express car and the tender.[2]

In this script, the basic trait of screenwriting is spelled out: the text is
written in the present tense, and it gives the impression that the action is
happening right now. Unlike the novelist who describes what has happened, the screenwriter describes what is happening. If the novelist tells
the story and "hears" the written words, the screenwriter presents the
story and "sees" the words.

Scene 3:   *Interior of express car.* Messenger is busily engaged. An
unusual sound alarms him. He goes to the door, peeps
through the keyhole and discovers two men trying to
break in. He starts back bewildered, but, quickly recov-
ering, he hastily locks the strong box containing the
valuables and throws the key through the open side
door. Drawing his revolver, he crouches behind a desk.
In the meantime the two robbers have succeeded in
breaking in the door and enter cautiously. The messenger opens fire, and a desperate pistol duel takes place in
which the messenger is killed. One of the robbers
stands watch while the other tries to open the treasure
box. Finding it locked, he vainly searches the messenger for the key, and blows the safe open with dynamite.
Securing the valuables and mail bags they leave the car.[3]

Thirteen (of fourteen) scenes of the script are united by the continuity of the action. As all screenwriters do to this day, Porter organizes his narrative by presenting events that happen simultaneously and by switching from one location to another naturally. The script ends with the robbers being "completely surrounded. A desperate battle then takes place, and after a brave stand all the robbers and some of the posse bite the dust." In the very last scene, an outlaw fires "pointblank at the audience" — just for the excitement of the public.

In its workmanship and completeness, Porter's script was a rare exception among the primitive, amateurish film stories of his contemporaries. Screenwriting at that time had neither traditions nor professionals. The pioneers of this new field were actors, newspaper journalists, and people from all walks of life.

The field was so young that one of the earliest American instructional handbooks on screenwriting had to explain what film was: "a celluloid strip about an inch wide, on which pictures are taken." It also provided a definition of a script: "Photoplay or Moving Picture play is a story told in pictures."[4]

The author recommended the minimal use of words to avoid filling the photoplay with "useless adjectives" (a remark that has not lost its freshness even now). He also recommended writing about "Integrity, Love, Friendship, Thoughtfulness, Charity, Devotion to Parents, Heroism, True Insight into Human Nature. . . . [and the] Foolishness and sure Punishment of Dishonesty, Selfishness and Cruelty" and advised against writing about burglary, kidnapping, suicide, or "other tragic subjects." "You can teach many good lessons, but no matter how sad your play may be, you must have a happy ending." There was also the caveat "Do not think you can write a play in an hour. Even experienced writers need a week often." Handbooks of this sort were more typical in America than in other countries and distinctions between the genres of screen texts were better defined. American film-writing professionals included specialists in the concise form of film treatment (sometimes called *scenario*), photoplay, and subtitles, yet screenwriting was not considered an important craft within the filmmaking industry. Many films were improvised either without any preliminary text or with just brief notes.

It is hard to believe now that D. W. Griffith shot and edited *The Birth of a Nation* (1915) and *Intolerance* (1916) without written scripts. Only for some of his films did he use a script, as he did for his short film *The New York Hat* (1912), written by one of the first American professional screenwriters, Anita Loos. (She was a master of subtitles, but Griffith usually preferred his own, overloaded and sentimental.)

The attitude toward screenwriting as an undignified profession developed in America in the silent era and, in a way, has survived to the present time. Interestingly enough, this attitude was shared not only by filmmakers and critics but sometimes by writers.[5]

The Russians and the Germans in the silent era, however, considered screenwriting a highly creative field. Sergey Eisenstein, for example, insisted that there be dynamic connections between the word of the script and the image on the screen. He was against what he called "the optical presentation of facts" in the script, be it reference to the position of the camera or to a description of the protagonist's appearance. The ideal script, according to him, should always be an inspiration for the director and should stimulate his creativity. Eisenstein even went so far as to insist that a script should resemble a work of poetry, thus neglecting to a large extent the script's most important quality—its concreteness.

Another celebrated Russian, Vsevolod Pudovkin, gave supreme importance to the script's dramatic organization and imagery. The screenwriter, first and foremost, must know how to select those objects and events that most express a particular idea visually ("plastically," as it was called by Pudovkin). Unlike Eisenstein, he believed in a structured film script, with every sentence having a precise visual equivalent.

But Germany was the country where the first truly accomplished scripts appeared. There, more than anywhere else, screenwriting, as well as film, was regarded in terms of and as part of the old artistic tradition not just as a new and alien phenomenon. Film was accepted as an art form equal to theater and painting, and screenwriting as a challenging literary genre. All the famous German directors of the silent era had their writers, whom they considered their respected partners. Fritz Lang worked with Thea von Harbou, Ernst Lubitsch with Hanns Krähly. Thus, *The Cabinet of Dr. Caligari* (1919), which has been called the most famous early film, is often said to be a film of Carl Mayer and Hans Janowitz, its writers, rather than of Robert Wiene, who was the film's director. It is known that Carl Mayer would take days to describe a few shots, a year to write a script, and would rather return an advance than compromise the quality of his work.

The original script for *The Cabinet of Dr. Caligari* has been lost; what is usually published as the script was made as a shot-by-shot description of the film. However, the script for an equally well known German film, Murnau's *Nosferatu, a Symphony of Horror,* has survived in its entirety. Its writer, Henrik Galeen, was influenced by Carl Mayer, and like him, he combined a great visual sensitivity with a clear, crisp writing style and a deep professional knowledge of every aspect of filmmaking.

The *Nosferatu* script has that poetic, inspiring quality about which Eisenstein spoke, but it also has Pudovkin's "cinematic plasticity" conceived in words.

Synopsis

A title announces that this tale is taken from the diary of a Bremen historian. The diarist wonders if Nosferatu was not responsible for the plague that struck the city in 1838 and tells the story of a young married couple.

In the early morning, Jonathon Harker, a handsome young man, admires his pretty wife Nina. The Harkers are obviously in love. They kiss passionately before Jonathon goes off to work.

Renfield, Harker's sinister boss, tells the young man that Count Dracula of Transylvania is interested in buying property in their city. He instructs Jonathon to leave at once for a meeting with the count.

Harker returns home and tells Nina that he must leave her for several months. He leaves his wife with their friends, Westenra and Lucy. Nina is grief stricken as Jonathon rides away on his horse.

Jonathon passes through the bleak, gloomy landscape of Transylvania. He stops at an inn and demands his dinner be served quickly so that he may be on his way to Count Dracula's castle. This announcement startles the several patrons at the inn. The owner warns Jonathon that he must not leave because "the evil spirits become all-powerful after dark."[6]

In his room, Jonathon reads *The Book of the Vampires* before going off to sleep.

The next day, Jonathon boards the coach that is to carry him the rest of his journey. He urges the driver to hurry, to get him to the castle before the sun sets. The driver refuses to go the whole way to Dracula's castle — "Not for a fortune!" He stops where the "land of phantoms" begins.

As Jonathon makes his way up the road that leads to Dracula's weird, forbidding castle, a coach draped in black curtains stops for him. The driver is also dressed completely in black. His face is hidden by his hat.

The driver points to the coach with his whip and Jonathon gets in. As the coach approaches the drawbridge to the castle, the driver stops.

As Jonathon approaches the doors to the castle, the gaunt figure of Nosferatu emerges from the shadows. He leads his guest into the dining room. Jonathon eats while Nosferatu reads a document. Jonathon is slicing a loaf of bread when the clock strikes midnight. Startled, he accidentally cuts his thumb. "Blood! Your precious blood!" exclaims Nosferatu. He seizes the young man's hand and begins to suck the blood. Horrified, Jonathon pulls his hand free.

When Jonathon awakens the next morning, he finds he is still in the chair he had sat in the night before. He notices that there are two small marks on his throat.

Jonathon goes upstairs to write a letter to Nina. From his window he notices a horseman passing and summons him. He meets the horseman halfway and gives him the letter to deliver.

In his room, Jonathon reads *The Book of the Vampires:* "Nosferatu drinks the blood of the young. . . . One can recognize the mark of the vampire by the trace of his fangs on the victim's throat." When the clock strikes midnight Nosferatu appears in Jonathon's room.

Meanwhile, in Bremen, Westenra sits at Nina's bedside and writes a letter, while the young woman sleeps. Nina silently rises from the bed and begins to walk in her sleep. When Westenra finally notices her, she is walking along the balcony railing. He catches her, just as she is about to fall. He calls to the maid to get a doctor.

Nosferatu's shadow creeps across Jonathon's face as he sleeps.

While the doctor and Westenra are looking over her, Nina springs up in her bed and with a dazed, blank expression on her face calls her husband's name. Nosferatu suddenly retreats from his would-be victim. The doctor attributes Nina's trances to "a sudden fever."

In the morning, Jonathon finds his way to Nosferatu's chamber. He struggles to open the heavy iron doors. He tears the lid off a coffin and runs away in terror when he discovers Nosferatu inside in corpselike repose.

Later, from the window of his room, Jonathon spies Nosferatu in the courtyard below. The vampire is loading coffins onto a wagon. Jonathon runs to the bed and begins to tear the sheet into shreds. He escapes through the window on a makeshift rope of sheets. Nosferatu slides into one of the coffins, and the lid mysteriously flies shut.

Two men are steering a raft loaded with Nosferatu's coffins. Meanwhile, in a hospital, a doctor tends to Jonathon. He is hysterical and tries to tell about the coffins, but the doctor and a nurse persuade him to rest.

A group of dockworkers are loading the coffins onto a ship, and they open the lid of one. The coffin is filled with dirt and crawling with rats. One of the rats bites a worker, and he beats at it with a shovel.

Renfield, Jonathon's boss and Nosferatu's agent, has been locked in a cell in an insane asylum—he is screaming for blood.

Nina, dressed entirely in black, wanders the dunes and gazes longingly toward the sea. Westenra and Lucy come running to her. They have the letter that Jonathon wrote, which promises his return. Nina clutches the letter to her heart and runs off.

Jonathon, who escaped the vampire's spell, is still weak but ready to leave the hospital. He thanks his nurse and staggers out of the room.

A ship moves swiftly across the sea, while Jonathon leads his horse down a wooded hillside.

Renfield filches a newspaper from the attendant who is cleaning his cell. The paper reports that a new plague has broken out, "attacking principally the young and vigorous. Cause of the two bloody marks on the neck of each victim baffles the medical profession." Renfield relishes the news and rubs his hands together like an insect.

Aboard the ship, all of the men but the captain and his mate have been stricken by "the plague." The mate takes up an ax and goes to inspect the hold. He begins to hack away at the coffins, and soon the hold is swarming with rats. Finally, he strikes the lid of the coffin in which Nosferatu rests. Terrified, the mate runs out of the hatch. As the vampire slowly heads toward him, the mate backs off in fear and, heedless of the captain's warning, falls backward over the railing. Believing that he is now alone, the captain ties himself to the wheel of the ship. He is trapped and panic-stricken as Nosferatu makes his way toward him.

Nina, in her room, can sense Jonathon nearing the city.

Renfield, in his cell, is extremely agitated about the arrival of his master. When the attendant comes into the cell, Renfield jumps him and escapes.

Nosferatu, carrying his coffin, arrives in Bremen with a swarm of rats following.

Jonathon and Nina have an emotional reunion. Nosferatu, wearing a sinister smile, spies on the couple before going on to his new house.

Westenra and a number of officials inspect the ship that carried Nosferatu. They discover the entire crew and the captain dead.

Westenra reads the captain's log in which the physical deterioration and deaths of the crew members, a possible stowaway beneath the decks, and the rats in the hold are described. The doctor takes the book away from Westenra, reads on, and proclaims that a plague has arrived. He warns everyone to stay in their houses.

The townspeople have obeyed the doctor's orders. Bremen appears to be deserted. People are slowly beginning to die. The rest live in mortal terror.

Against her promise to Jonathon, Nina reads *The Book of the Vampires*. She learns that only "a woman pure in heart" can break Nosferatu's spell.

A vigilante group chases Renfield through the town. He cackles madly as he eludes them.

Nina rises from her bed as Jonathon sleeps in an armchair by her bedside. She throws open her windows and looks across at Nosferatu's house. Nosferatu, from his window, stares hungrily in her direction. She opens her arms invitingly. Nosferatu moves from his window. Nina goes to Jonathon and shakes him. As he awakens, she faints. He lays her on the bed and rushes out of the room. Nina returns to her window, but Nosferatu is no longer at his. He suddenly appears before her in the stairwell. She is terrified and backs away as Nosferatu approaches. He backs her onto the bed. Meanwhile, Jonathon is at the doctor's house, trying to rouse him from his sleep.

Nosferatu is at Nina's throat.

A cock crows the arrival of the new day. Renfield, now in his cell, jumps up in alarm. He rants and screams a desperate warning to his master. He is finally subdued by the attendants.

Nosferatu holds his chest in pain as he tries to make his way from Nina's room. In vain, he tries to shield himself from the sun's rays. He is rapidly weakening. He vanishes, leaving a faint cloud of smoke in the sunlight. Tightly bound in a straightjacket, Renfield sadly announces his master's death.

Nina awakens just as Jonathon and the professor arrive. She is weak but wears a peaceful expression. She dies in Jonathon's embrace.

"And at that moment, as if by a miracle, the sick no longer died, and the stifling shadow of the vampire vanished with the morning sun."

The script by Henrik Galeen, like any other film script, is not the final product; it is a stage in the creation of a film. Nevertheless it gives the impression of a complete literary work: its text is clear, rich in images, and creatively condensed. "We are looking at an ancient house through panes of glass; it is six or seven storeys high, with arched windows open; it exudes a sombre, death-like atmosphere."

For the screenwriter, it is more important to find an image ("a sombre, death-like atmosphere") than to go into detailed description. And Galeen presents many images: the "ghostly glow of a candle"; a raft swept away by a turbulent river; "a fog-shrouded street" with a man who lights a large lantern. When he mentions a single ray of sunlight, which gets into Nosferatu's castle through a crack in the window, it is not just a ray of light, it is an image, a reminder of the goodness that finds its way into even the world of evil.

The alternation of light and shadow has a symbolic meaning in the script. Jonathon's and Nina's house, with flowers in front, is brightly illuminated. Nosferatu's castle is dark and full of shadows—the vampire is associated with the night, and he dies at the first ray of the morning sun.

Dark-light images appear quite often in the script. Sometimes they are just details without direct relation to the development of the action. Yet they are valuable devices in creating a certain emotional atmosphere: a white spider against a dark background, "busily enticing a victim into a web"; or Nosferatu's black-draped coach, passing through "ghostly white" trees.

Nosferatu is an archetypal film script in its lucid style of narration. "The shadow of Nosferatu, hunched with claw-like hands at the ready, appears in the stairwell." The lean sentences look more like the lines of a poetic text than like those of a functional text. "The skeleton on top of a clock strikes a glass chime: it is midnight."

Nosferatu was one of the first scripts to set an example of character description. The author does not write much about Jonathon, only that he is young. The rest—that he is in love and loved, that he is devoted to his job, that he is not a coward—the reader gathers from his actions. The same is true for "his pretty wife," Nina. The reader comes to know her through the action. Nothing is mentioned about her face, eyes, or figure. The reader knows only that Nina is "pure in heart," which is the only point that matters for the purpose of the narration—the rest is the work of the director.

However, Nosferatu and especially his assistant, Renfield, are described in more detail. Nosferatu's appearance must inspire fear and revulsion. The script details his "terrible," tall, thin figure; his "sinister form" and "singular appearance"; one reads that he "makes a strange, almost inhuman movement with a long, tapering hand, flicking it up to his brow and down again"; that he has pointed ears, a misshapen skull, hollow eyes, fangs, bushy brows; that he wears a bulky coat, which fits high up around the back of his neck.

The description of Nosferatu is a part of the dramaturgy of the script. Without this sense of otherworldly ugliness, one could not fully comprehend the revulsion and terror experienced by Jonathon or the sacrifice made by Nina.

But the most detailed description is that of Renfield, Jonathon's sinister boss and Nosferatu's devoted agent. The reader learns from a subtitle inserted into the text that "the agent Renfield was a strange man, and there were unpleasant rumors about him"; that he is "a shrivelled, old man"; that he is "bald, with bushy white eyebrows and a band of hair around the back of his head"; that "he holds his head slightly on one side, mouth open"; that when he smiles he "flashes his bad teeth."

The author pays particular attention to Renfield because the details of this character are important for the action. He is a semivampire in disguise. His appearance, his habits, his manners are all part of the plot. Only by knowing them can one visualize a scene in which he loses his mind after sensing Nosferatu's approach. "Renfield . . . snatches at the air with one hand, sucks at the other; then he begins to grin sinisterly and moves slowly across the room with his left hand extended in front of him. . . . Renfield moves slowly towards the two astonished observers, his hand held above his head, then suddenly makes a determined leap for the throat of the supervisor."

Each successive sentence in the *Nosferatu* script moves the action forward.

The skeleton figure on the clock strikes midnight on the glass chime.

Jonathon suddenly jumps up and hides the book behind him, and moves to another part of the room.

Jonathon walks to an arched door, opens it slightly, looks through, but jumps back involuntarily.

At the end of a dark hallway stands the terrifyingly cadaverous figure of Nosferatu, eyes gleaming.

In this kind of narration, the transitions from one episode to another are free and flexible. There are no stylistic bridges—every new image is just a new line on the page. This organization of the text is very cinematic, similar to film editing: joining pieces of film footage back to back that have differing location, action, and mood.

In his narration, the author describes on paper the film that he is "seeing" in his mind. Although the camera is never mentioned and there are no instructions to the camera, its presence is always sensed. One notices it in the shifting points of view of the camera—now very close to its object, now far away.

> We see Nosferatu's house across the street. [long shot]
>
> Nina continues to gaze through the window, apparently in horrified fascination. [medium shot]
>
> The shadow of Nosferatu, hunched, with claw-like hands at the ready, appears in the stairwell. [long shot]
>
> Nina. . . . Her eyes dilate with horror as she looks at what is coming from the stairs. [close-up]
>
> The shadow of Nosferatu, hand extended, moves across the wall. [long shot]
>
> Nina backs to the bed, then pulls herself up on to it. [medium shot]
>
> In the dim light of Nina's room, Nosferatu's head can just be seen close to Nina's throat. [close-up]

Galeen's narration from time to time does provide an indication of where the camera should be placed (the angle of the shot), but he uses no technical terms.

While reading about the sudden appearance of Nosferatu in front of the ship's captain, the reader "sees" the vampire from a very low angle— he "appears ominously above a hatch."[7] He looks the most sinister and frightening from this position. When Nosferatu is "placing a coffin on a horse-drawn wagon, on which two coffins have already been placed," the reader, together with Jonathon, watches the action, looking down into the courtyard from a high window somewhere under the roof of the castle. The high angle, by including more space and showing more of what is going on, makes the scene even more horrible.

In some passages, one can sense the movement of the camera, for example, when "Nosferatu appears in the doorway, somehow becoming larger and larger until he fills the doorway completely." The camera moves closer and closer to the vampire. This gradual movement gives more intensity to the action.

From time to time the screenwriter conducts two or more parallel actions, constantly switching from one to another.

> Jonathon runs along by the front, many-windowed wall of a house. . . . he stops and calls out.

> Nosferatu carries his [own] coffin. . . . he stops in the shade of a tree.
>
> Jonathon is. . . . clasping his fainted wife to him.
>
> Nosferatu stands looking at Jonathon's house.
>
> Jonathon and Nina hug each other closely.
>
> Nosferatu turns and looks up, smiling subtly.

This simultaneity is typical of film. The ability to conduct several lines of action—sometimes parallel to each other, sometimes intersecting, other times wandering far apart, but still concurrent—is one of the most important skills of the screenwriter.

Silent films worked out their own relationship to words. Most of these techniques would later lose their usefulness for the talkies. Nevertheless, the model of economy in film dialogue was formed at that time.

Nosferatu, a classic silent film script, has all the variations of titling: *subtitles,* often called *captions* or just *lines; inserts,* any written words that appear in a movie—a letter, a poster on a wall, a page of a book; *intertitles,* the text of a film's prologue or epilogue or remarks by the author projected on the screen.

Subtitles are used economically in the script. The author knows that they can be employed only where visual images cannot convey the needed information. For example, subtitles appear in the beginning of the script when Jonathon's boss, Renfield, tells him about the impending business trip: "Here is an important letter from Transylvania. Count Dracula wishes to buy a house in our city"; or when the Transylvanian driver says to Jonathon, "We will go no further, sir. Not for a fortune. . . . Here begins the land of phantoms." In addition to supplying information that is essential for the plot, subtitles in the script can foreshadow coming action, as when Renfield addresses Jonathon, "You will have a marvelous journey. And, young as you are, what matter if it costs you some pain—or even a little blood." We immediately become intrigued. What will happen? What could cost Jonathon "a little blood?"

Sometimes a subtitle can be very intense, working as a powerful dramatic accent: "Dinner, quickly! I should be at Count Dracula's castle," cries Jonathon to the innkeeper, whereupon all the other guests recoil from him in horror. They know about the phantoms and the count, but he does not. The same effect is achieved when Nosferatu sees Jonathon cut his finger with a knife and exclaims, "Blood! Your precious blood!"; or when Renfield, panic-stricken in his cell bed, sits up, raises his arms, and cries out, "Master! Master! Master!"

Galeen sets an example of concise dialogue, trimmed of excess wording. He uses subtitles sparingly, knowing that every subtitle, being static by nature, inserted into a film halts the action.[8]

In contrast to dialogue in films with sound, subtitles seldom differentiate the speech of one character from another. The subtitles are so condensed and simplified that there is no room for such refinements; Nosferatu's speech is no different from Jonathon's or from the doctor's. "You are late, young man. It is almost midnight. My servants have all retired."

In the script, there are also several inserts—quotations from Jonathon's letter to Nina ("Nina, my beloved—don't be unhappy. Though I am away, I love you"); newspaper headlines ("New Plague Baffles Science"); pages from the captain's log (18 May 1838—Passed Gibraltar—Panic on board—Three men dead already—Mate out of his mind—Rats in the hold—I fear for the plague"); and from *The Book of the Vampires* ("and it was in 1443 that the first Nosferatu was born"). Especially important is the insert from *The Book of the Vampires* that says, "Only a woman can break his frightful spell—a woman pure in heart—who will offer her blood to Nosferatu and . . . will keep the vampire by her side until after the cock has crowed." This insert gives dimension to Nina's character and explains the importance of her sacrifice.

Intertitles in the script include the written prologue, "From the diary of Johann Cavallins, able historian of his native city of Bremen: "Nosferatu! . . . Was it he who brought the plague to Bremen in 1838," and the epilogue, "The sick no longer died, and the stifling shadow of the Vampire vanished with the morning sun." The two placards are like parentheses that contain the narration. Aside from these instances, the narrator's voice breaks in only occasionally either to explain something or to push the action along.

Modern film dialogue developed largely from the dry, often naive, matter-of-fact subtitles and intertitles of silent films, rather than directly from theatrical dialogue. In general, a play is based on the word, a film on the visual image, which silent films demonstrated convincingly.

As mentioned earlier, *Nosferatu* was one of few scripts of the 1920s to possess such cinematic and literary completeness. Only with the appearance of sound, and consequently, dialogue, did the silent-era scripts mature and turn into the screenplay—a more complex and developed form.

2.
Script Composition

La Strada
by Federico Fellini and Tullio Pinelli, with Ennio Flaiano

La Strada, 1954
  Director: Federico Fellini
  Screenplay: Federico Fellini, Tullio Pinelli, with Ennio Flaiano

The highly artistic, exuberant, mysterious, and witty films of Federico Fellini (b. 1920) are filled with autobiographical details, childhood memories, and his personal fascinations. *Amarcord* tells of Fellini's boyhood days in the Italian seaside resort of Rimini. *I Vitelloni* contemplates his postadolescent years' loafing about in this same town. *Roma* reminisces about his move from the province to the capital. *8½* is a representation of the intellectual and emotional intensity of his existence as a film director. *The Clowns* shows his lifelong obsession with the circus. *A Director's Notebook* and his last film, *An Interview*, document Fellini's inspirations and experiences in a straightforward, documentary format.

Fellini began his career in film as a screenwriter in 1944, when he met the director Roberto Rossellini. The two collaborated on the script for *Open City,* which proved to be the seminal film of Italian neorealism. Over the next few years, Fellini would work as a screenwriter and as an assistant director to Rossellini and to a number of other directors before going on to make his own films. After two poorly received productions, he had his first success with *I*

Vitelloni in 1953. But it was in 1954 that he scored what was perhaps his greatest achievement, *La Strada*.

The script for *La Strada* ("The Road") was written by Fellini along with Tullio Pinelli and Ennio Flaiano, two of his most frequent cowriters. The plot was mainly developed by Fellini; Pinelli brought to the script his observations on the life of wandering performers and gypsies, and they both agreed that *La Strada* would be about human solitude and the inability of people living together to communicate. The writer Ennio Flaiano joined Fellini and Pinelli when the first draft of the script had been completed, and his main role, in his own words, was to "say derogatory things about *La Strada* for three months. . . . I condemned a vagueness of atmosphere, certain affectations in the characters, and I insisted that the story, though very beautiful, should come down to earth and that the symbolism should be integrated with the narrative."[1] According to Flaiano, only at the final stages of shooting and editing *La Strada* did Fellini find a balance between the true world of the road and the poetic world of his imagination.

La Strada established one of Fellini's favorite themes, the individual's quest for the meaning of existence, set against his most fruitful subject, the circus. The film starred Giulietta Masina, Fellini's wife. Her portrayal of the simpleminded clown Gelsomina is a cinematic classic in its own right and a touching tribute to Charlie Chaplin. The parable-like story confused some critics, and Fellini's courageous humanistic concern for the individual caused others to see it as a betrayal of neorealism, with its typical emphasis on societal problems.

La Strada became an international success but only gradually. Shown first at the Venice Film Festival of 1954, the film was received cautiously and was awarded a Silver Lion. Giulietta Masina received no awards at all. It was not until a year afterward that the film was fully recognized in Europe and in America. It played for three years in New York and garnered the first of Fellini's four Oscars. "With *La Strada* . . . I was at peace with myself and with my pride as an artist,"[2] wrote Fellini. "*La Strada* will remain the crucial point in my life." In this film, Fellini expressed all that he could "weep for, laugh, suffer or hope for."[3]

In the past thirty years, Fellini has implanted in audiences' imaginations his aesthetics, his peculiar visual world. "Felliniesque" is already an international adjective used to describe something bizarrely disproportionate and delicately balanced between the ugly and the beautiful. It is true that in recent years his films have seemed less inspired (for example, *Ginger and Fred*), yet Fellini's reputation rests securely on the indelible inventiveness of his earlier achievements and, most of all, on *La Strada*.

The word *composition* in the original Latin means bringing parts together into a unified whole. The composition of a poem, symphony, painting, building, or film does precisely that. It establishes order and organization, a specific arrangement of parts and elements. It is often this order that makes the work of art so pleasing. Composition stands in striking contrast to the constantly changing, often chaotic process of life. It is made from real-life material yet is organized, complete, and thus satisfying.

There are no written rules for achieving composition. From time to time, in different periods of history, some rules were formulated and accepted as a necessary norm. In the fifth century B.C., for example, the Greeks calculated what they believed to be the ideal numerical proportion between the human head and the body in sculpture and the ideal correlation between the columns and the rest of a temple; in the seventeenth century, the French created the canon of classical tragedy, which demanded unity of space, time, and action. These rules of composition were maintained for a time and then rejected by following generations. Yet, even rejected, in cultural traditions they remained supreme examples of organization and order.

There is a certain universal, innate understanding of artistic composition. Even if one were to compare a Greek temple, a classical symphony, a film, and a simple quilt, one would find some similarities in their basic designs. Each has a planned, not arbitrary, structure; each achieves a balanced unity by both direct and subtle interplay among the parts and between the parts and the whole; each also has the common principle of repetition—variation and development of the same motifs throughout the entire work.

Composition may be accidental, as in pottery (where the results of glazing often cannot be predicted), or spontaneous, as sometimes in painting or song. But even there one finds balance, proportion, and rhythm—the alternation of powerful and light strokes, bright and subdued spots, vigorous and melancholic lines, sharp and soft sounds, extended and brief musical or ornamental passages.

Film shares the principles of composition common to all the arts, but it also contains some principles that are specifically its own. The whole as the unity formed from the parts is, perhaps, more evident in film where individual frames constitute a shot, shots come together in a scene, scenes are united into a sequence, and sequences, in turn, compose the film. Film is one of the most complex arts, and film composition is a system in which action, speech, music, visual images, and light affect, influence, and depend upon each other.

The chief function of script composition is the development of the story, characters, and action. In itself, script composition is complex. It organizes the scenes, their sequential order, and their mutual interdependence. It brings together the character development and the action—from the opening to the climax to the resolution. (Some of these aspects of script composition are discussed in other chapters.) To illustrate the organization of scenes in a script, what binds them together, what is emphasized or inferred, and how the arrangement of the scenes—the composition—expresses the central idea of a film, Fellini's *La Strada* is used as an example.

Synopsis

Gelsomina, a simpleminded girl, walks along the beach with a bundle of reeds tied to her back. Her little sisters run up to her, calling her home: "A man is over there with a great big motorcycle!" He is Zampano, the strongman. He is looking for a girl to replace Rosa, Gelsomina's sister, who has just recently died while traveling with him. Zampano looks Gelsomina over with some obvious doubts, nevertheless settles for her, and gives her mother some money. Gelsomina runs to say goodbye to the sea.

Gelsomina sits nearby watching as Zampano performs his strongman stunts in a crude circus ring for a crowd in a provincial Italian town. The crowd cheers and applauds. Gelsomina passes the hat.

Later, at their camp, Zampano gives Gelsomina some of Rosa's old clothes and starts to teach her how to beat a small drum and call out, "Zampano is here!" Each time she fails to do it right, he lashes her with a switch.

At night, Zampano calls Gelsomina into the trailer to sleep with him. Later in the night, Gelsomina is crying and smiling while Zampano snores loudly.

Gelsomina bangs the drum as Zampano performs his stunt, and then they clown together to the delight of the audience.

At night, Zampano and Gelsomina are eating in a tavern. She is happy. Zampano spots a buxom, red-haired prostitute, finds her rather appealing, and drives off with her. Gelsomina is left on the road.

The next morning, Gelsomina is sitting sadly by the curb. A local woman tells her of a strange man asleep near a wagon in a field on the outskirts of town. Gelsomina hurries there to find Zampano alone and asleep. She is afraid that he is dead and almost cries.

Zampano and Gelsomina are part of the entertainment at a country wedding reception. Gelsomina dances for a group of children. Secretly, they lead her to a room in the attic of the farmhouse, where a retarded child sits in bed alone. Gelsomina tries in vain to entertain him.

Meanwhile, Zampano is devouring a plate of spaghetti and talking to an older woman. She offers Zampano some of her late husband's clothes, and he leaves with her to "try them on."

Zampano returns to the barn where Gelsomina is waiting and brags about his new suit. He does not notice her sorrow at all.

As Zampano is sleeping, Gelsomina leaves the clownish outfit he has given her, gathers her things, and escapes into the early morning.

Gelsomina is sitting by the side of a deserted country road, when a small band of musicians marches by. As if hypnotized by their music and their rhythm, Gelsomina follows them.

High above the crowd, wearing a small pair of angel's wings, the Fool, a tightrope artist, rides a unicycle. He sets a table and eats a plate of spaghetti on the tightrope. He pretends that he is falling but catches himself and performs some graceful swings. The audience, and Gelsomina particularly, are astounded.

That night after the festival, Gelsomina haunts the nearly deserted square. Suddenly, Zampano drives up and orders Gelsomina into the trailer.

In the morning, Gelsomina awakens to discover that she is in the midst of a camp where a circus is being set up and that they are in Rome. She comes upon the Fool, playing a sweetly sad song on his little violin. Zampano and Gelsomina are hired to work with the circus.

Zampano later in the circus ring begins his act with the chain. Just as he is building his act to its overdramatized climax, the Fool, seated in the audience, tells him that he is wanted on the telephone. The crowd roars with laughter. Furious, Zampano chases after the Fool but is unable to catch him.

The next day, Gelsomina admires the Fool as he practices his act. He begins to teach her a few steps and some notes on the trumpet. The manager is watching approvingly and considering the possibility of a new act featuring the Fool and Gelsomina. When Zampano discovers this scene, he is enraged and announces that Gelsomina will work only with him. The Fool taunts him, inciting his rage once more. The Fool throws a bucket of water in Zampano's face, and Zampano chases him with more fury than before. He has chased the Fool into the back room of a café and now is brandishing a knife and trying to break down the locked door. The Fool is trying to escape through a window when the police arrive. Back at the circus, the owner tells Gelsomina that both men have been taken to jail and that he does not want to have either of them around anymore.

The circus camp is soberly quiet that night. The tents are partially dismantled. Gelsomina is confused and cries.

The Fool appears, and she talks to him about Zampano and herself. He says that perhaps Zampano loves her, and perhaps her purpose is to stay with Zampano. Gelsomina is content now. The Fool drives Gelsomina to the police station to wait for Zampano. The Fool is about to leave. He takes a little chain he has around his neck, hands it to Gelsomina, and goes away singing her name playfully. From the back of the trailer, she waves goodbye to him with tears in her eyes.

The next morning, when Zampano is let out of jail, he finds Gelsomina waiting for him, and once again they are on the road. They stop along the shore. Gelsomina is excited as she runs toward the water. She asks Zampano to point to where her home is. "Now my home is with you," she tells him proudly. He reacts in his usual way.

A pretty young nun rides along in the trailer with Zampano and Gelsomina. They stop at her convent, and Zampano asks if he and his wife may spend the night there. The mother superior agrees to let them stay in the granary. The nun brings them some supper, and in gratitude, Gelsomina plays a lovely song on her trumpet. Even Zampano seems to be a little moved.

That night, as they are about to go to sleep, Gelsomina asks Zampano if he would be sorry if she were to die. She begins to tell him that every little stone has its purpose, but he goes to sleep.

Gelsomina is awakened in the middle of the night to discover that Zampano is attempting to rob the sacristy. He tells her to help him. Horrified, she refuses to do it and Zampano beats her.

The next morning, Gelsomina and Zampano prepare to leave. The young nun notices that Gelsomina is unhappy and offers to let her stay at the convent, but Gelsomina refuses. The nun understands. "You follow your husband, and I follow mine," she says. Gelsomina cries and sadly waves goodbye as the trailer rolls away.

As they ride along, Zampano spots the Fool by the side of the road fixing a flat tire on his car. Zampano pulls the motorcycle over and approaches him. Zampano is as angry as ever and begins to fight. The Fool tries to defend himself, but Zampano overpowers him. He bangs the Fool's head on the fender of the car and stomps away. The Fool is dazed. "He broke my watch" is all that he can mutter as he tries to walk. He stumbles and falls down. Gelsomina runs to him crying, "The Fool is hurt!" Zampano realizes that he has killed the man and in a frenzy throws the Fool's body into a nearby stream. Then he pushes the Fool's car into the stream.

Later, Zampano performs his routine before a small gathering. Gelsomina is oblivious to her cues. She wanders about, mesmerized, repeating to herself, "The Fool is hurt."

It is winter, and it has snowed. Zampano and Gelsomina are on the road once again. He pulls the trailer to the side of the road. Gelsomina disembarks and walks away in a trance. There are signs of concern on Zampano's face. When he asks her if she would like to go back to her mother, she does not answer. She does not even seem to hear him. Sitting by the fire, Gelsomina refuses the food that Zampano offers her; at night, she makes him sleep outside on the ground.

Some days later, in the morning, Gelsomina looks recovered. Zampano is quite relieved. He tells her that the Fool's death was an accident, which reawakens her sadness. She weeps and mutters, "The Fool is hurt." Zampano offers again to take her back to her mother. She goes to a sunny spot and lies down. She whispers that she must do as the Fool said and stay with Zampano. She falls asleep wearing a strangely peaceful smile. Zampano rushes to the trailer and gets some blankets to cover her. He quickly gathers his belongings from the camp and hurries back to the trailer. He finds Gelsomina's trumpet and quietly goes to leave it at her side along with some money. Zampano pushes the trailer quietly along the road. When he is at a safe distance, he starts the motorcycle and speeds away from the sleeping Gelsomina.

A parade is marching through a small town. Zampano plods along. He looks much older, tired, and troubled. Suddenly, he hears a woman's voice humming Gelsomina's sad tune. He sees a young woman hanging her laundry. She tells Zampano that she learned the song from a girl her father found several years ago on the beach. She never spoke and seemed crazy. The girl has since died, the woman says.

At the circus ring, Zampano goes through the same routine. His enthusiasm has faded completely.

Later that night, Zampano is in a local tavern, very drunk. The owner and several patrons have to throw him out into the street. He is furious, throwing garbage cans and empty crates at the door. "I don't need anyone!" he shouts into the empty street.

Zampano finds his way to the beach, staggering, and wades into the water. He walks back up the beach, kneels in the sand, and faces the sea. He looks up at the sky. A sob fills his chest and shakes him all over.

Zampano is weeping.

Recently published in English, the continuity script of *La Strada*[4] describes every one of the 745 shots in the film, including the distance of the camera and the camera movements.[5] For example:

507. LS: the van, as it comes to a halt beside the road. Overcome by an intense sense of excitement, Gelsomina climbs out of the van and, as she touches the ground, she races away from the van to the right a short distance along the coastal road. Camera follows. Then she stops and runs back to the van. Camera tracks left to her and Zampano in LS, then pans on Gelsomina, leaving Zampano out of frame, as she races toward the sea. Camera then halts and frames her in ELS.

508. MCU: Gelsomina in right profile. She remains motionless and still with her gaze fixed upon the expanse of sparkling water.

509. MS: Zampano reaches the water, removes his shoes, and rolls up his pants.

510. MS: Gelsomina, back to the camera, still gazing at the sea.

511. MS: Zampano, back to the camera, still rolling up his pants.

GELSOMINA (off): Which way is my home?

Compare the continuity script fragment to the original in Fellini's and Pinelli's script.

EXT BEACH SUNSET

The road under the moving motorcycle emerges along the dunes . . . onto the seaside. The sea is wide and luminous.

ZAMPANO has already dismounted, and is moving slowly toward the water.

GELSOMINA overwhelmed by an intense excitement, runs straight ahead on the coastal road, barely touching the ground; she stops, runs in a different direction, stops again, as dogs do, when trying to recognize a place. . . . She turns back hurriedly, runs toward the sea, reaches it before ZAMPANO does. In her haste she goes a few steps into the water with her shoes on. She lets out a small, stifled shout; jumps back up onto the sand; stays still, immobile, her gaze fixed on the shimmering stretch of water.

Meanwhile ZAMPANO has reached the shore; he pulls off his shoes, rolls up his pants, slowly wades into the sea, stopping when the water reaches his calves. For a while nothing is heard except the noise of the waves and the wind. Then GELSOMINA, staggered, dazed, asks:

GELSOMINA
Which way is my home?[6]

Along with the setting and dialogue, a certain mood is expressed in this scene.[7] Any mention of the technical aspects of the scene would destroy it by cluttering the clear, direct line of the story.

Screenwriters do not think in terms of shots; the *scene*—the smallest segment of narrative—is the basic unit of the screenplay. For example, in *La Strada*, there is the opening scene with Gelsomina at the sea shore; the scene in which Zampano kills the Fool; and the last scene, with Zampano crying. A scene happens in unbroken time and usually in one space. It is united with some related scenes into a *sequence*—a larger script-film unit analogous to an act of a play or a chapter of a book.

The scenes of the original *La Strada* script are conjoined into fourteen sequences. To every one of them Fellini and his coauthors gave a detailed heading:[8]

1. For about ten thousand lire, a strongman, Zampano, buys a half-witted girl named Gelsomina and takes her away from her family.
2. Gelsomina's awakening. Zampano's work. Zampano as Gelsomina's teacher. Night falls. Gelsomina is Zampano's woman.
3. Gelsomina's debut. Zampano takes her to dinner in a real restaurant, then leaves with another woman. Gelsomina's solitude as she waits all night and all day.[9]
4. Zampano's awakening. Gelsomina's tomatoes. On the road.
5. "The artist's life." The music that makes Gelsomina cry. Gelsomina's homesickness. Again on the road.

6. Gelsomina and Zampano perform on a prosperous farm. Zampano makes love to an older woman for a hat and a blue suit. Gelsomina's loneliness at night when she tries in vain to talk to Zampano.
7. Christmas time approaches. Gelsomina's flight. Her arrival at a village festival. Gelsomina for the first time sees The Fool who flies above the crowd. The disastrous adventure with some drunken soldiers. Zampano takes Gelsomina back with him. They resume their journey together.
8. Gelsomina and Zampano become contracted to the Colombaioni Circus. The Fool and Zampano do not get along. The Fool plays an ancient song for Gelsomina.
9. A fierce fight between Zampano and The Fool. Zampano is in prison. The night time conversation of Gelsomina and The Fool.
10. Gelsomina and Zampano in the "Saber Act." The sea. Gelsomina's melancholy as she recalls her home and plays the ancient song on her trumpet.[10]
11. The convent. Gelsomina's conversation with a young nun. Night. Gelsomina asks Zampano if he loves her. Zampano wants to rob the sacristy.
12. Zampano kills The Fool. Zampano's flight from village to village with Gelsomina, crazed with sorrow.
13. Conversation between Gelsomina and Zampano.
14. Many years later. Gelsomina's song. Zampano finds out that Gelsomina is dead. Zampano gets drunk. Zampano's solitude and lament.

The sequence headings included in the finished script of *La Strada* are summaries of the action in the sequences.[11] Screenwriters usually weave similar webs with two- or three-sentence summaries of sequences in their notes while in the process of structuring their scripts. They balance long sequences against short ones, noisy and populated ones with quiet ones, tense dramatic ones against tranquil or funny ones.

La Strada is simple on the surface, but it has many layers of meaning in its essence. It is a twentieth-century parable about a brute, a holy fool, and a simpleminded girl who, according to Fellini, is "both a little crazy and a little saintly." Street performers, they live on the margins of society, existing on their own, subjects to no one, living as only beggars and kings can. They have no home, and their life is nomadic: the road, then a stop, then the road again.

Fellini expresses this pattern of existence in the very composition of *La Strada*—in the contrast between the dynamic nature of the road, with its constantly changing sights and surprises, and the static nature of Zampano's performing the same act (breaking the iron chain) again and again. The repetition of this act—sequences 2, 3, 6, 8, 13, and 14—gives the whole composition a distinct rhythm, which can be visualized in the following figure, wherein a circle stands for a performance and parallel lines, the road.

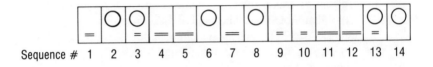

Sequence #   1   2   3   4   5   6   7   8   9   10   11   12   13   14

In sequence 2, Zampano confidently enters a circle of curious villagers for the first time in the script. He tells them about the dangers of his attempt to break the iron chain with only the expansion of his chest muscles, wraps the chain around himself, kneels on the ground, inflates his chest, and bursts the massive chain. The theme of Zampano's might—his almost animal-like physical strength—and the monotonous routine of his act is introduced. Variations on this theme appear further on.

In the next performance, sequence 3, Zampano is kneeling again, in the center of a circle formed by some other villagers, straining, inflating his lungs, and breaking the chain. But Gelsomina's presence turns Zampano's act into a cheerful performance. With her comically painted face and bowler hat, she enthusiastically beats the drum: it is her debut. Even Zampano now looks satisfied and calls her his wife: "my wife will pass a hat around later." He adds an amusing comedy number to his old monotonous act. Sporting a funny fake nose, Zampano plays a hunter, and Gelsomina, waving her little capelike wings and quacking, portrays a duck. The hunter shoots her, and he himself falls down from the loud report, playfully and euphemistically foreshadowing the whole story. The delighted crowd applauds.

The theme is an allegro variation of the stated theme. This mood continues in the next performance, at the country wedding (sequence 6). Although prior to this point Zampano has abandoned Gelsomina on the road, leaving with a prostitute and returning much later, Gelsomina has no memory of evil. With tambourines and bells, oblivious of herself, she struts back and forth to the music surrounded by the village children. This performance is an expression of herself, her own act of creation. While it is tense and burdensome to look at Zampano's act, it is joyful and easy to watch her movements.

Between this stop and the next in sequence 8, Gelsomina witnesses a miracle—a performance by the Fool (sequence 7). At night, in the beam of a spotlight way up above the ground, the Fool, with his little wings, is balancing on a rope suspended across the piazza. His performance is a dazzling combination of mastery, danger, and the thrill of toying with that danger.

Nothing could be further removed from the world of Zampano, whose next act is presented in a circus arena (sequence 8), several months later. It follows immediately the performance of the Fool, who swoops down from the cupola of the tent and lands gracefully on a donkey standing in the center of the arena. And then, as though nothing special has happened, he proceeds to clown around with the other performers. Zampano's pompous entrance into the area, his speech about the expansion of his "pectoral muscles" and about his chain being made of pig iron, his grave promise to shatter the hook, his invitation for the audience to check that this hook is real, and his mention of the grave danger of this act are all given the appearance of being pathetic and small by comparison with the grace of the Fool's performance. This variation of the theme takes on a grotesque form. When Zampano, his lungs full of air, is about to break the chain, the Fool, seated in the audience, calls out that Zampano is wanted on the telephone. There is a burst of laughter. Zampano's act is now the object of ridicule. The playful mind of the Fool instantly defeats Zampano's muscular might.

The next—the fifth—repetition of Zampano's act occurs in sequence 13 after he kills the Fool in sequence 12. Once again there is the same pacing around the ring. This time the arena is a village square on a gray winter day. There is Zampano's same warning: "If there are any squeamish people in the audience, I'd advise them not to look. The hook can rip into my flesh and some blood might spill. The drum will roll three times. If you please, Signorina Gelsomina." Gelsomina in her bowler hat stands obediently with her drum, but the sticks dangle in her hands. In a silent frenzy, staring straight ahead, she repeats, "The Fool is hurt." Now the variation of the theme becomes tragic.

The sixth and final performance (sequence 14) takes place several years later. Zampano has just found out about Gelsomina's death. He enters the ring and, as always, walks around it. He does and says all the same things. But his energy is gone. The crowd watches indifferently as Zampano kneels in the center of the ring. In this final variation, the theme exhausts itself.

Not every sequence includes the road, and the road does not always constitute the greater part of a sequence. Nevertheless, it is the dominant image of the film. It is always there, literally, symbolically, or both.

On the simplest level of the plot, where the road has its direct meaning, Zampano and Gelsomina are riding along the road, as do all other traveling comedians and circus performers, including the Fool. The road is their home (so naturally, Gelsomina sleeps by the side of the road, covered with a blanket).

Every road leads somewhere—also both literally and symbolically. The next level of *La Strada* associates the road with life itself—the road of life; the road as a calling, as chance, as fate. *La Strada* brings Gelsomina and the Fool to their deaths and Zampano to his awakening.

In his composition, Fellini avoids smooth linkage of events. It is not a stream of life that he presents but a performance of selected episodes. Now crude, exaggerated, or paradoxical; now tender or mysterious; their combination leads one to understand that the longest and most winding road is the one that lies between Gelsomina and Zampano.

Contrast is one of the primary devices Fellini uses to compose sequences or the scenes within them. Night and day, different seasons, traveling on the road and performing, comedy and tragedy are alternated.

Right after Gelsomina's debut, in sequence 3, the "duck-hunter" act, the first and only understanding between her and Zampano, there is a sudden complete distancing in their conversation:

GELSOMINA: Where do you come from?
ZAMPANO: From my part of the country.
GELSOMINA: Where were you born?
ZAMPANO: (Sneering) In my father's house.

In the farm scene (sequence 6), the revelry of the wedding in the yard below stands in opposition to the silence and isolation in the bare little room high up in the attic where Gelsomina, along with the children who brought her there, tries to cheer up the semiparalyzed boy, Osvaldo, "as pale as a white mushroom," who is an expression of loneliness even deeper than Gelsomina's. In sequence 7 after the quarrel with Zampano, Gelsomina falls into a hole (literally the lowest point); in a later scene within the same sequence, the Fool is performing high above the ground (the highest point). The scenes of the nuns' kindness in the convent in sequence 11 are followed by the murder of the Fool in sequence 12.

But the main contrast in *La Strada* is between the Fool and Zampano. They are opposites in every respect—the lightness, almost weightlessness, of one and the bulk of the other; virtuoso mastery versus brute strength; fragile delicacy versus crude survival; wit versus surly dullness; little wings versus pig iron chains; the Fool balances in the air, while Zampano, breaking the chain in his act, becomes almost rooted to the ground. The Fool and Zampano represent opposite elements — air versus earth — and Gelsomina's realm, in turn, is the sea.

The sea is shown three times in the film at the most revealing moments in the plot (sequences 1, 10, and 14). At the beginning of *La Strada,* Gelsomina is seen by the sea — she was born there and lives there in a shack by the water. Before leaving with Zampano, she runs to its edge to say goodbye. In this sequence, the sea has its concrete, direct meaning as an environment.

The next time water is seen (sequence 10) is after Gelsomina realizes that her life has a purpose. "Before, I wanted only to go back there. . . . Now it seems that my home is with you." The sea to which Gelsomina now runs is much more than a place or an environment. Its shimmer and its animated motion express Gelsomina's excitement.

Her whole being is so in unison with the sea that when it appears for the third and final time (sequence 14), it brings to the reader (and to Zampano, too) the image of Gelsomina, even after she is long gone. Now the sea is shown by moonlight. Zampano, on the shore, raises his eyes to the sky and weeps. On the level of reality, Gelsomina was defeated, abandoned, and left to die on the road, but on the spiritual level, she has won: because of her, Zampano's humanity now awakens within him.

The three sea sequences help the reader understand that every sequence of *La Strada,* as in other well-written scripts, is an essential part of the screenplay's entire composition and that the sequences are bound together not only with the obvious development of the action but also with the deeper ties of moods, associations, similarities, and contrasts.

3.
Opening, Climax, Resolution

The Servant
by Harold Pinter

The Servant, 1963
Director: Joseph Losey
Screenplay: Harold Pinter

Joseph Losey (1909–84) studied medicine at Dartmouth and English literature at Harvard before he went to New York in 1930. There he worked as an actor and staged the first variety shows at Radio City Music Hall. In 1935, he traveled to Moscow, where he participated in some of Eisenstein's film classes. When he returned to America, he worked on documentary shorts and in radio, as well as on the stage. Losey cited Bertolt Brecht as a strong early influence on his career. He directed Charles Laughton in Brecht's *Galileo Galilei* after World War II, with the dramatist himself serving as advisor on the production. Losey adapted this work to film in 1971. The play was so successful that RKO Pictures offered Losey the chance to direct his first feature film, *The Boy with Green Hair*, in 1948. It would be the most popular of the handful of films that Losey made in America.

In 1951, Losey's career in Hollywood was cut short when he was blacklisted for refusing to testify before the House Un-American Activities Committee. He went to England, where his first few features were released under a pseudonym, Joseph Walton, to protect their standing in the American market. He was established as a director of international importance.

Losey scored his most outstanding successes with films that were scripted by Harold Pinter: *The Servant, Accident,* and *The Go-Between.* In Pinter, Losey found someone who shared his cynical view of the world and his sophisticated and detached sense of drama.

Harold Pinter (b. 1930) is one of the most famous contemporary British playwrights. He began his career on the stage with the Royal Academy of Dramatic Arts and had been acting for ten years when in 1959 his first play, *The Caretaker,* established him as a natural dramatist. Pinter abandoned acting almost completely and went on to write some of the most noteworthy British plays of the past twenty-five years.

Pinter has lent his talent generously to screenwriting. Aside from his work with Losey, he has also written the scripts for *The Pumpkin Eater, The Last Tycoon,* and *The French Lieutenant's Woman,* among others. He is a master of form, often approaching the screenplay as a work of art.

The Servant was adapted from the Robin Maugham novella of the same name. It premiered at the Venice Film Festival in 1963, where it was coolly received before going on to more successful runs in Europe and America. It was nominated for the British Oscar for best picture the following year.

Although Pinter sometimes likes to discuss screenwriting as though it were improvisation and spontaneity, his own screenplays are meticulously structured and stylized; *The Servant* is a good example.

In the majority of film scripts, plot development depends on three points: the *opening,* when, where, and how the action begins; the *climax,* the highest point of dramatic tension; and the *resolution,* how the script ends, the denouement of all dramatic conflicts and contradictions. These points were not invented by theoreticians. Screenwriters inherited them from a centuries-old tradition of storytelling.

A story about an event—whether told by an ancient chronicler or by a friend—almost always moves from its beginning upwards to the climax of the action. Soon after this point comes the resolution. The following is a simple example.

"Three youths walked up to a respectable old man on the subway, surrounded him, and demanded money from him. However, he refused to give them any." The conflict begins. It arises out of the opposing desires of the characters.

Now the dramatic tension depends on how the conflict will be resolved, on what happens at the climax. In this story, the dramatic tension depends upon who will gain the upper hand. "The youths moved closer and closer to the man. Suddenly, two of them pulled out knives." This is a crisis, a confrontation, which changes the course of the action and the balance of power.

"Then the old man unexpectedly drew a revolver" — which is yet another crisis and moves the action further along — "and shot the three youths." This is the highest or most intense point in the development of the story, the final crisis — the climax. It develops from and in response to the main conflict and a series of crises.

When a storyteller or a screenwriter begins a narration, the climax of the story is prominently in mind. The teller concentrates on how to approach it in an intriguing way, how to make the climax more unpredictable and surprising. If the youths had walked up to the man simply to ask him what time it was, there would have been no story.

The climax is usually followed by a resolution — the denouement, the fall of the action, although sometimes the plot will break off at the climax if everything has already been said. "After the man shot the youths, he jumped through an open door onto the platform and became lost in the crowd. The three youths remained lying on the floor of the subway car."

What if the end of this story were to be altered? Suppose the youths wore masks, and suppose the man shot two of them, the third jumped from the car, the man jumped after him, and shot him in the back. When the youth fell down, the man ran up to him and tore the mask from his face. It was his own son. Now this moment, not the shooting, is the climax. The climax of the first version of the story becomes, in the second version, just one of many crises. Here, the scene in which the father recognizes his son is the most important crisis, which resolves the drama and is the climax.

It is always helpful to view the development of a plot graphically as a kind of triangle, in which the angles represent the opening, the climax, and the resolution.

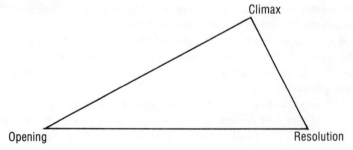

This simple drawing illustrates the ascent to the climax and the descent from the climax to the resolution. Often the term *resolution* is used not only for the very end of a script but also for the entire descent from the climax to the end. The closer to the end of the film the climax occurs, the sharper the descent to the resolution will be.

Sometimes when screenwriters develop a plot for a script they graph the crises schematically.

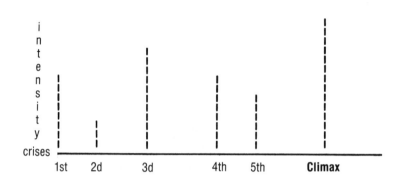

Any graphic representation of the plot helps the screenwriter develop the script. Here, for example, the height of each vertical bar corresponds to the intensity of the crisis. In fact, the very process of making graphs and geometric drawings is natural for screenwriting because it is not so much writing as building and structuring. First the plot is constructed, and only afterwards is the construction described.

Do all screenwriters make drawings and diagrams? Surely not. Not all of them. Not always. For experienced professionals there is often no need to draw the structure on paper. They feel it intuitively. But in the process of learning how to write a script, it is helpful to make graphs and diagrams to see the whole composition and the exact *triangle of plot*. If a screenwriter starts a script without structuring it first, just by writing separate scenes, thinking that they can be somehow fit together later, it will not work. It would be like building a house without a blueprint.

The Servant by Harold Pinter is an example of a highly structured plot in which the opening, the climax, and the resolution are put together in a sophisticated manner. Discovering their dependence on each other is a challenge.

Synopsis

In response to an advertisement, Barrett, a middle-aged man-servant, arrives at the house of Tony, a young London aristocrat. Tony has just bought this house and now needs a servant. Barrett appears suitable, and Tony hires him.

Barrett looks after the house, organizes the renovation of every room, and personally redecorates them. He anticipates Tony's every wish. But in his obliging manner, there is something cynical, almost sinister.

Tony meets Susan, his fiancée, in an elegant restaurant. He tells her about a project he wants to participate in: building three cities in a jungle in Brazil. Intelligent and sharp, Susan is skeptical about his plans. But it does not really matter—she is in love with him.

Susan comes to see the new house. She meets Barrett. When the servant leaves the room, Tony praises him. He says that he has never been more comfortable in his life. Susan, however, dislikes Barrett.

The couple visit Tony's elderly friends, Lord and Lady Mountset. In a casual way, they discuss Tony's Brazil idea. No one except Tony seems enthusiastic about it. Lady Mountset is sure that the peasants in Brazil are called "ponchos."

With Tony's consent, Barrett hires a cleaning woman, Vera. Barrett presents Vera as his sister. In fact, she is Barrett's lover.

Tony and Susan are in a small French restaurant in Soho. Somehow, the conversation turns to Barrett. Susan says that the servant is loathsome. Tony gets upset and says that she "got the whole thing absurdly out of proportion."

Barrett, meanwhile, is ready to do anything to get rid of Susan. He realizes that Tony and the house can "belong" either to him, or to her. He incites Vera to seduce their master. Barrett leaves for a day, supposedly to visit his mother, and Vera succeeds. Tony spends a night with her. Now he is obsessed with Vera and tries to avoid Susan.

Once while Tony is out, Susan arrives with some flowers and small pillows she has bought for the house. She is openly hostile towards Barrett.

Tony and Susan spend a weekend at the Mountset estate. They are together again on a snowy winter day. They decide to leave the estate earlier than they had intended so they might spend the night in Tony's house in the bedroom "with the best view."[1]

Their car pulls up to the house. The bedroom windows are brightly lit. Barrett and Vera are in their master's bed, drunk, and they do not hear Tony opening the front door. Vera berates Barrett for his "bloody smoking." Barrett berates Vera for asking for constant lovemaking and for being like a "bloody machine."

Barrett, almost naked, appears in the bedroom doorway. "She is your sister, bastard!" Tony shouts. "She is not my sister, Sir," Barrett replies. "And if I might say so, we are both rather in the same boat." Barrett makes the latter comment for Susan's benefit.

Tony throws Barrett and Vera out. Shocked, Susan leaves.

A few weeks later, Tony is drunk, unshaven, and alone in his now untidy house.

In a pub, Tony runs into Barrett. The servant begs for another chance. Vera has left Barrett and has taken all his money. "She was to blame. . . . she done us both," he says.

The house is the same, though darker, more oppressive, and more untidy. The curtains are drawn. Now the master and the servant are two fighting lovers.

Vera arrives and asks Tony for money. Barrett throws her out.

"Your old flame," Barrett informs the drunken Tony when Susan comes to see him. Tony and Barrett are expecting guests. Susan tries to talk to Tony. She says that she still loves him. He does not listen. "Join the party," he answers.

At the party, several drunken women, Vera among them, surround Tony. One of the women throws him on the bed and falls down with him. "We are going to Brazil in the morning," jokes Barrett. Susan, in confusion and despair, moves toward Barrett and kisses him. Tony gets up off the bed, but he falls down pulling the tablecloth, dishes, food, and wine off the table. Then he gets up and smashes the record player, which has been playing his and Susan's favorite record. "Get them all out!" he shouts.

Barrett pushes the women out. "You too!" he yells at Susan. He leads the other women to the front door.

Susan slowly goes down the stairs, walks up to Barrett, and with all her might, slaps him across the face.

Barrett recovers his composure, goes to the front door, and holds it wide open. Susan leaves the house.

The servant closes the door, locks it, and goes upstairs to Tony.

In the beginning of the script, Barrett walks to Tony's house to apply for a job as a manservant.

Exterior. Knightsbridge Square. October. Day. A great square off Knightsbridge. Winter sun. Bare trees. Numerous parked cars.

> At the far side of the square Barrett appears. From high, see him approach. . . . His steps are sharp on the pavement.

By the way Barrett advances toward Tony's house ("his steps are sharp on the pavement") and because he is seen from above and because of the laconic dynamism of the description of the whole scene, Pinter creates an energetic opening. Barrett, proceeding toward Tony's house, is reminiscent of a well-aimed cue ball at the beginning of a game of billiards: it spins across the table and will, in a second, strike and scatter all the other balls.

The door to Tony's house is unlocked and Barrett enters. "No sign of occupation. Silence." In one of the rooms, in an old deck chair, Tony sleeps covered with his coat. "Too many beers at lunch," he explains, awakening.

The script could have started differently: with Barrett already working for Tony; with the death of Barrett's previous master; with Tony buying the house; or with Tony first meeting Susan. One can imagine a great many openings for *The Servant,* but the author presents the opening that provides the best introduction to and lays the foundation for the development of the main ideas of the drama: how the servant becomes the master.

When comparing *The Servant*'s opening with its resolution, it becomes clear that the author crafted the idea skillfully. In the opening, the door is unlocked, which corresponds to the beginning of the action—opening the door and entering; in the resolution, Barrett locks the door—the action is resolved, "closed." In the opening, the house is empty; at the end, there is a chaos of things thrown around and upset on the floor. In the opening, the servant's steps "are sharp on the pavement"; in the resolution, "he walks slowly up the stairs." In the opening, the master makes the following statement:

> TONY: I'll need . . . well, everything (he laughs). General looking after . . . you know.
>
> BARRETT: Yes, I do, sir.

The resolution brings an unexpected grotesque meaning to these words. Barrett really does do everything.

For the reader, a script starts with the first scene, but for the author, the first scene is only the border between the script and what has happened before. Because the author knows what has happened to the characters in their prescript lives, the first scene is just the moment at which the story and the characters are revealed. The author must figure out at what moment to open their lives to the readers.

When the reader sees Barrett moving toward Tony's house at the opening of *The Servant,* nothing is known about his motives. Only two people know — Barrett himself and Harold Pinter. The author knows Barrett's past and present, his tastes, his family, where and when he was born, and how he acquired his lust for power. Pinter also knows Tony in detail (he created Tony thoroughly), and he knows why Tony needs someone to control and direct his life. Barrett's and Tony's past histories, although not included in the plot, determine all aspects of their present behavior.

From the past histories of the characters — sometimes called the *backstory*[2] — the author brings into the script only a few carefully chosen facts and details, most of which provide information necessary either for plot development or for character development. For example, Barrett was a manservant to Viscount Barr, whom Tony's father knew well, and both of them died recently, "within a week of each other." The viscount's death explains why Barrett now needs a job. It also emphasizes Tony's belonging to high society and Barrett's subservience to that society.

Some other facts and details from the past, the prescript life of the characters, make them more three-dimensional and, therefore, more believable. Thus, even a minor remark, that the armchair in which Susan is sitting was once Tony's mother's favorite chair, sends us back to Tony's past, giving the character more history. From the script, the reader learns also that both Barrett and Tony have served in the army.

BARRETT:	You know sometimes I get the feeling that we're old pals.
TONY:	That's funny.
BARRETT:	Why?
TONY:	I get the same feeling myself. PAUSE.
BARRETT:	I've only had the same feeling once before.
TONY:	When was that?
BARRETT:	Once in the army.
TONY:	That's funny. I had the same feeling myself there, too. Once.

This information implies that a camaraderie, owing to a similar experience, exists between Barrett and Tony. It also expresses the uniqueness of their current relationship, which involves and evokes emotions rarely felt by either character. It comments on the environment they have created: an isolated existence; a world, as "once in the army," without women.

The opening sets the mood of the whole film. Nothing dramatic happens here, yet some of the author's remarks — about the emptiness of the house, about the winter sun falling across the floor, about the slight echo that words gain there—create a disturbing atmosphere.

In the opening of *The Servant,* the two main characters are introduced to the audience and to each other. Barrett, after walking through the empty rooms, stops and stands above the sleeping Tony. "Low down in an old deck chair lies a body. . . . Barrett approaches, stops a little way from the body, regards it." Tony is sleeping "low down"—the author hints at Tony's weakness and vulnerability. Describing Tony, the author uses the word "body" twice: "lies a body" and "from the body"—as if a corpse were being described. Barrett attentively examines the sleeping master, looking down on him from above—the reader receives the impression of superior energy and alertness on the part of the servant.

This contrast suggested in the script is carried further in the film by its director, Joseph Losey. In the film, Barrett comes out of the shadows. He is completely dark, with dark clothes and dark hair; Tony, sleeping near a glass door to the garden, is all light, with light clothes, light hair, and almost childlike face.

A little later, Tony and Barrett discuss the servant's responsibilities: "Barrett sits. Barrett's chair is in the center of the room. Tony, while speaking, moves about the room, almost circling the seated figure." Here, the author, just by describing the mise-en-scène, expresses the strength and composure of the servant, who sits steadily in the center, and the weakness and discomfiture of the master, who circles around him.

In the opening, Pinter introduces another character—the house itself. The reader sees it in various conditions and moods during the course of the drama: completely empty; ordered and well maintained; inviting; untended; a shambles; and ultimately sinister. The house, with its dark, shadowy corners, physically unites the master and the servant and finally entraps them. The house also attracts both men to itself. At one point, Barrett mentions that he misses the house. Tony longs for the house and then at the end cannot and does not want to part with it. Neither the master nor the servant can separate himself from the house. Tony says he is "damn lucky" to have gotten the house. He also mentions several times that he is lucky to have the servant: "Damn lucky to get this place, actually. Little bit of wet rot, but not much. Sit down" The house has "rot," a subtle, almost unnoticeable, but significant detail. Being rotten characterizes Barrett's, and eventually Tony's, personality. But the author uses it only in reference to the house.

The "wet rot" along with the unlucky number thirteen (introduced when Barrett mentions that for the last thirteen years he had been a manservant to various members of high society) are the author's hints at the presence of evil in the air in the film's opening.

The ascent to the climax always begins with the establishment of the conflict. The conflict of *The Servant* may appear at first to be between Susan and Barrett. They detest each other from their first meeting. In fact, Susan is against Barrett even before they meet. As they lie on a rug in the living room, Tony tells Susan about Barrett. She treats the idea of having a manservant as a joke.

> Tony kisses her.
> SUSAN: Bachelor. (She kisses him.)
> TONY: Oh, by the way, I forgot to tell you. I've found a manservant.
> SUSAN: (laughing) What?

Notice that the theme of the manservant, which begins with Susan's ironic laughter, ends at the resolution with her tears and fury.

When Tony introduces Susan to Barrett, the latter offers to take her coat. She refuses. She wants nothing to do with Barrett. He, in turn, treats Susan with disinterest and disdain. When they discuss the furniture in the house, Barrett lectures her, saying that a simple and classic style is always the best.

> She looks at a heavy ornament.
> SUSAN: It is classic? This isn't classic, it's prehistoric.

Of course their disagreement cannot end on this humorous note: the true object of their struggle, Tony, is too important to both of them. As Tony becomes more and more involved with the servant, he unwittingly reinforces Susan's dislike for Barrett.

> TONY: He's been a wonderful help, that chap. Wait till you taste the food. Honestly, I've never been more comfortable.
> SUSAN: Never?
> TONY: I don't have to think about a thing.
> SUSAN: Does he give you breakfast in bed?
> TONY: Of course.
> She smiles faintly, stands, walks about.
> SUSAN: Have you checked his criminal record?
> Barrett appears at the door.

At this point, their confrontation is already established.

Susan and Barrett are diametrically opposed to one another. Barrett is dishonorable and has a lackey's viciousness. Susan is straightforward and content with her life. He belongs to the circle of servants, she to that of masters. But they share a common goal: they both want to control Tony and each is jealous of the other. They both know that Tony has no will, that he is an alcoholic, and that either one of them is stronger than he is.

Gradually Barrett advances, and Susan loses one point after another. When Barrett decorates the house, Tony thinks it is perfect, and the servant tries to lecture Susan. Barrett knows how to cook, while she, presumably, does not. At one point, Tony says, "Women are no damn good. They can't cook." Tony becomes rapturous at dinner over Barrett's long white gloves, though he never gets excited about or even notices Susan's clothing.

From passive competition, Barrett moves to active competition. He clears the room of the flowers that Susan brought. He steps into the room as if by accident when Tony and Susan are making love. He brings Vera into the house, not so much for himself as to get Tony away from Susan and to let him fall as low as possible, thus beginning the process of moral decay from which there can be no return.

The confrontation between Barrett and Susan—a crisis—becomes serious when she, feeling that Tony's feelings have cooled (but knowing nothing about Vera), drops by the house with flowers and some cushions to reaffirm her position and presence in Tony's life. Tony is out. Susan openly and maliciously displays her hatred for the servant. She consciously belittles him with the tone of her orders. And when she is apparently asking his opinion about the flowers and the little pillows she has brought, she turns the question into humiliation.

BARRETT: I beg your pardon?
SUSAN: What do you think of the cushions?
BARRETT: It's difficult to say what I think of them, Miss.
SUSAN: Shall I tell you the truth, Barrett?
BARRETT: Yes, Miss.
SUSAN: The truth is, I don't care what you think.

She goes further by rudely asking Barrett if he uses any deodorant. Finally, she asks him the question she has wanted to ask him all along.

SUSAN: What do you want from this house?
BARRETT: Want?
SUSAN: Yes, want.
BARRETT: I am the servant, Miss.
SUSAN: Get my lunch.

The change in the development of the action happens when Tony and Susan unexpectedly return home and find Barrett and Vera in the master bedroom. Although Tony chases Barrett out of the house, the servant still has the upper hand. He and Tony are involved with the same woman, they "are both rather in the same boat." Susan is a witness to this scene.

Through the vulgar exposure of his infidelity, Tony has lost his self-respect, the respect and trust of his fiancée, and he may have lost Susan altogether. Barrett is victorious, and his conflict with Susan is now resolved. Barrett may be thrown out of Tony's house, but Susan looks like a fool. She has not succeeded in controlling either Tony or the house. While this scene resolves the conflict between Barrett and Susan, it is not the climax, it is only a crisis. At this point, Barrett's victory over Susan, the result of the drama and the future plight of the characters is unclear; therefore, it is a confrontation that changes the course of the action but does not resolve it.

While at first glance the main conflict in *The Servant* appears to be between Barrett and Susan, it is not. The central conflict arises between Barrett and Tony.

After his dismissal, Barrett runs into Tony at a pub and begs to be given "another chance." Their relationship begins to move along a new path. This step, in fact, becomes another on the road of the master's moral decay, aided by the servant. In the opening, the author foreshadows this development when Tony walks up to the window and looks out at the gardens in the square while talking with Barrett. Barrett's reflection appears in the window. Barrett literally stands between Tony and the world and distorts Tony's "picture of the world."

After Barrett returns to work for Tony, everything in the house changes. "It is airless, dark, oppressive. Curtains and blinds are almost completely drawn. There are no longer any flowers. There is an overlay of Barrett everywhere. Photos of footballers cellotaped to mirrors. Pornographic calendars. Nudes stuck in oil paintings."

The master is now under the complete control of the servant. Only rarely are there outbursts reminiscent of Tony's former status and haughtiness: "You're a servant"; "You're supposed to be the bloody servant"; or of his fury: "You filthy bastard"; "Now leave my house alone." However, these eruptions quickly turn into apologies and supplications. The servant has attained power. Scenes of vulgar scandals—"Take your pigsty somewhere else"; "You creep"—alternate with idyllic scenes of their dinners together—"Fabulous"; "It's marvelous."

Barrett forces Tony to serve him. He humiliates his former master. He behaves like a malicious and quarrelsome wife: "Why don't you get yourself a job instead of moping around here all day?" Through drugs and alcohol, Barrett ensures his control over Tony. He makes sure Tony's glass is never empty of liquor. He obtains drugs for Tony: "Something special from a little man in Jermyn Street." Even when they play hide-and-seek, Barrett manipulates and torments Tony with guilt. "You are hiding, but you'll be caught. You've got a guilty secret. . . . I am coming to get you," screams Barrett. Tony and Barrett are now lovers. The author alludes to this very unambiguously. Their homosexuality (bisexuality), however, is in no sense the center of this drama. This relationship is simply another expression of Barrett's power over Tony. Now the threat of the appearance of a mistress for the house has been all but eliminated.

Understanding the complex conflict of *The Servant* is not easy. There is one scene in the script that serves as a metaphor for this conflict. The scene takes place on the central staircase of the house. Tony and Barrett are playing a ball game, the rules of which they have invented. Barrett is at the foot of the stairs, Tony at the top.

BARRETT: What about me? I'm in the inferior position. I am play-
               ing uphill. . . . There's no need to take advantage of
               the fact that you're in the best position. . . .
TONY: My dear. . . . My dear Barrett, you're just a little upset
               because you're losing the game.

First Barrett throws the ball at Tony. Tony throws the ball back just as viciously as the servant threw it at him and hits Barrett in the nose. Barrett screams and clutches his nose. Tony runs to him in fright.

TONY: Now look . . . Listen, I am grateful, honestly. . . .
               Don't be daft. You know I am. I don't know what I'd
               do without you.
BARRETT: Well go and pour me a glass of brandy. . . . Don't just
               stand there! Go and do it.
Tony runs into the drawing room and pours Barrett a large brandy. Barrett watches him from the hall.

The master is too weak willed, alcoholic, spineless, and irresponsible to face the situation squarely. He cannot bear to be alone. He needs someone to take care of him at all costs, even at the price of his self-esteem.

The servant despises and envies Tony because Tony is the master and he is a servant. He wants revenge neither for reasons of material wealth nor for want of social justice. His is a metaphysical revolt, a revolt by someone who is not in "the best position" — "at the top of the stairs," so to speak — against someone who is. His is the passion of the lowly to be on the same level as the superior. To raise himself up is impossible; to drag Tony down is the only remaining alternative.

Barrett isolates Tony from the world and from any possibility of redemption. Tony does not go out of the house at all. Only once he mentions, dreamily, going for a walk. Tony sinks lower and lower, and Barrett goes down with him. He secures his power over Tony, corrupts him, and sinks with his master, becoming a drunkard in the process. "I am a gentleman's gentleman, and you are no bloody gentleman," declares Barrett. Being a "gentleman's gentleman" is not only a profession to him but also his social status. And if his master is no longer a gentleman, it means that he — the servant — is a nobody.

In *The Servant,* the climax occurs during the orgy scene. Barrett has invited some women to the house. Unexpectedly, Susan drops in. She has not seen Tony since the scandal with Barrett and Vera. "I love you. . . . Don't you . . . like me at all?" she asks Tony. "What's wrong with me then?" Tony leads her out to the other guests, who include Barrett, four women, and Vera. Tony asks Barrett to give him a drink. He does. "Do you want one, love, eh?" Barrett asks Susan.

> A girl pulls Tony gently away. . . .
> A woman in a large black hat pulls him down on the bed and kisses him.
> BARRETT: (to Susan) Do you know where we're going in the morning?
> PAUSE.
>   We're going to Brazil in the morning. (He grins) Aren't we Tone? (To Susan) Have a fag.
> Tony lies on the bed staring glazed at Susan. Susan moves to Barrett and kisses him. He laughs and holds her. She looks at Tony.

Whether Susan kisses Barrett to make Tony jealous or to draw herself nearer to him by sinking to his level is not important. That Susan's kiss confirms servant and master have become interchangeable is important.

While she kisses Barrett, Susan looks over at Tony: "his mouth is open, he moves from the bed." This movement is but a momentary stirring of honor (he goes up to Susan to protect her; she represents his past, the time when he still had some dignity). But this impulse dies as quickly as it flared up. "He shivers, stumbles, falls and collapsing, brings tablecloth, glasses, bottles down with him."

Tony is finished. The main conflict of the screenplay—the struggle between Tony and Barrett—is resolved with Barrett's complete victory. This point is the climax of *The Servant*—the strongest crisis bringing the drama to an end.

Everything that happens after the climax is the resolution. Tony shouts: "Get 'em all out." Barrett escorts the drunken women to the door saying, "Make it tomorrow night. . . . And bring John," and chases Susan out. She hits Barrett "with all her might . . . across the face" and leaves. The drama has ended. Barrett, Tony, and the house remain alone.

The concept of the *triangle of plot,* the rise to a climax and the fall to a resolution, can sometimes organize individual sequences as well as the entire script. To review, the *scene* is a group of shots related to each other mostly by the same location; the *sequence* is a group of scenes related to each other by an event or an idea. The largest unit within a film, the sequence, is a substantial, self-contained segment of film narrative.

In *The Servant,* there are 137 scenes and 33 sequences. Some sequences are short and consist of only two or three scenes. Others are much longer and more fully developed dramatically.

In one sequence, the action takes place mainly in a restaurant in Soho. The theme of jealousy and suspicion develops in the conversations of four separate, unacquainted couples. Very short scenes with Barrett and Vera (a fifth couple) are inserted several times into the restaurant sequence: Barrett meets her at the station, they are then in the car. Barrett and Vera do not utter a single word, but their intermittent presence gives the sequence dramatic substance. The closer Barrett and Vera get to the house, the more intense becomes the struggle between Tony and Susan in the restaurant. Pinter interrupts the restaurant scenes with those of Barrett and Vera as aggressively as the servant himself has interrupted every rendezvous between Tony and his fiancée.

The sequence has eight scenes. In the following description of the scenes in the sequence, notice that every other scene belongs to Barrett and Vera:

Scene 1   Barrett is standing on the platform waiting for Vera.

Scene 2   Tony and Susan meet at a French restaurant in Soho. At one of the tables, a girl and a man are talking jokingly about someone who is "a wonderful wit." The girl "is dying" to see him again. "You won't for some time," the man answers. "He is in prison."

The headwaiter recommends that Tony and Susan try the roast duck. Susan gives Tony a present.

For the time being, everything is very peaceful and loving between them. However, a reminder of a third person is indirectly introduced in the conversation between the girl and the man. Between Susan and Tony there is always this "third" present either physically or in spirit. They are never truly alone together. The mention of jail in the conversation between the man and the girl, coupled with the baseness of their conversation, calls forth a feeling of something impure and dishonorable, something associated with Barrett.

Scene 3   Vera and Barrett. She is running down the platform toward him.

Scene 4   Tony and Susan are eating. Another pair—a bishop and a curate—enter the restaurant.

Scene 5   Vera and Barrett walk down the platform not talking to each other.

Scene 6   Tony and Susan are eating in silence. Near them, another couple—a middle-aged woman and her young woman companion—are arguing heatedly.

OLDER WOMAN:	What did she say to you?
YOUNGER WOMAN:	Nothing.
OLDER WOMAN:	Oh yes she did. She said something to you.
YOUNGER WOMAN:	She didn't. She didn't really.
OLDER WOMAN:	She did. I saw her mouth move. She whispered something to you, didn't she? What was it? What did she whisper to you?
YOUNGER WOMAN:	She didn't whisper anything to me. She didn't whisper anything.

Here too, an absent, third person disturbs the relationship of these two lovers. The tone of their argument creates an atmosphere of suspicion, ambiguity, and jealousy. Even though at this point Susan and Tony are discussing something very peacefully, it is a reminder of their own disagreement.

Scene 7   In a taxi, Vera and Barrett "are sitting, not touching." Vera looks out the window.

Scene 8   Tony and Susan are having coffee. The bishop is
talking to the curate and criticizing some "third"
person. The curate does not agree.

Their conversation continues the theme of discord and suspicion begun by the two women. Now Susan picks it up: "I just don't
like him," she says, without even mentioning Barrett's name. "You
don't know him," says Tony. [The line of the triangle moves up-
ward toward the highest dramatic point of the sequence.] "I don't
trust him." "Why?" [It moves still higher.] "You have got the whole
thing absurdly out of proportion." The bishop takes this theme of dis-
trust to a new level:

BISHOP: And where are you creeping off to now, my
son . . . ah?
CURATE: Nowhere, your Grace, nowhere . . . Nowhere at all.
BISHOP: Is that a fact?

The theme continues, and Susan takes it further. "Why don't
you just tell him to go," Susan demands. "You must be mad," answers Tony indignantly. This insult, a behavior that is foreign to
Tony, the explosion, is the highest point of the sequence.

But the quarrel goes no further. Susan does not confront Tony,
and this argument does not resolve her conflict with Barrett and
consequently with Tony. It follows, then, that this episode cannot
be the climax, although it is similar.

Now comes a calming of the action as it moves downward to
the resolution. The man and the girl from scene 2 discuss a gift he
gave to her (stockings, perhaps). "They are gorgeous — absolutely
gorgeous. . . . Divine, but I simply couldn't get them on."

"I am sorry," admits Susan. "Well . . . Well, I wouldn't,"
says Tony. And he touches her hand, "frowning, unsure."

Not every sequence can be or needs to be so highly organized and
have a structure similar to the entire script. But some do, and they also
contain the distinct triangle of plot, with a well-defined opening, climax,
and resolution.

4.
Character Development

The Godfather
by Mario Puzo and
Francis Ford Coppola

The Godfather, 1972
  Director: Francis Ford Coppola
Screenplay: Mario Puzo
            Francis Ford Coppola

Francis Ford Coppola (b. 1939) is one of the wave of directors who emerged from the prestigious American film schools in the 1970s. He studied at UCLA and later worked as a director under Roger Corman and as a screenwriter on several successful projects. His screenplay for *Patton* won an Oscar in 1970.

Coppola was only thirty-one when Paramount Studios offered him the job of directing *The Godfather,* after several well-established directors had turned it down. The studio wanted a low-budget film, produced quickly, to cash in on the extraordinarily popular Mario Puzo novel. Coppola's film turned out to be neither low budget nor quick. First, Coppola convinced the studio executives to more than double his two-million-dollar budget. Then he managed to procure, against the arguments of the Paramount executives, Marlon Brando for the title role and a cast of then relative unknowns for the supporting roles (Al Pacino, Robert Duvall, James Caan, Diane Keaton, Talia Shire, and Richard Castellano). Once it was underway, the production was plagued with unforeseen difficulties. In response to a mutinous attempt by his editor and by his assistant director to have him replaced, Coppola had them fired. Vic Damone, who was originally to play the Johnny Fontane character, backed out of the film because he thought it presented a negative view of Italian-Americans. The Italian-American Civil Rights League raised six hundred thousand dollars to stop production of the film for the same reason. To quell their protests, the producer promised to remove all references to the Mafia and to Cosa Nostra from the script—a shrewd move since neither expression ever appeared in the script. However, despite the walkouts, protests, bomb threats, rallies, and letters to Congress, or perhaps because of them, *The Godfather* was a box-office hit. The film instantly earned the place that it holds in the history of American cinema. It won the Oscar for best picture in 1973.

Coppola followed *The Godfather* with three more films of distinctive quality, *The Conversation, The Godfather II,* and *Apocalypse Now.* He has turned much of his attention to entrepreneurial endeavors, his independent production and distribution company, and has produced films by other directors and secured the distribution rights to many foreign releases. Some of his directorial efforts have been botched by a too technically innovative approach, but with his most recent film, *Peggy Sue Got Married,* Coppola seems to have rediscovered his concern for narrative.

The Godfather was scripted by Coppola and Mario Puzo (b. 1929), although Robert Towne *(Shampoo, Chinatown)* had an uncredited rewrite of several scenes. According to Puzo, their method was peculiar: he wrote one-half of the script and Coppola wrote the other, then they traded and finished each other's work. Puzo's novel had skyrocketed him to success even before the production of the film. Because of it, he bore a hefty share of *The Godfather's* controversies. Owing to the vividness of its characters and their underworld milieu, many people assumed that Puzo had Mafia connections. At one point during the script writing, an indignant Frank Sinatra publicly chided Puzo for the Johnny Fontane character, a washed-up, sycophantic pop crooner, whom Sinatra took quite personally. Puzo pleads innocent to all the accusations leveled against him. He claims to have written *The Godfather* to pay off some debts and to enable himself to write the books that he wanted to write.

The novel was one of the most successful paperback sellers of all time; nothing that Puzo has written since has been quite as popular. Nevertheless, with *The Godfather,* Mario Puzo has given the cinema the most profound gangster story ever filmed and has most probably been able to pay his debts.

In one of Nikolay Gogol's (1809–52) plays, *Marriage,* a capricious young woman, having to choose among several unsatisfactory suitors, wonders why there could not be a man who had the nose of one, the mouth of another, the worldliness of a third, and the impressive physique of a fourth. As ridiculous as this may sound, it is precisely what a screenwriter does when conjuring up characters. The screenwriter intricately combines, in one individual, the qualities of several different people — real and imagined. From a multiplicity of traits, the screenwriter chooses a few that are essential to the plot; each character must serve a function within that plot. No character exists on his or her own.

Screenplay characters — main, major, and secondary — reveal themselves through action and dialogue. They are not given a broad range of attributes, and their descriptions are usually laconic. But, it goes without saying that the main character, the protagonist (a story can have more than one protagonist), is among the screenwriter's foremost concerns. Everything about the character — face, build, height, smile, speech pattern, walk, facial expressions, mannerisms, gestures, talents, intellect, moral code, sexual preference, attitudes, outlook, vices, idiosyncrasies, interests, ambitions, profession, income — and everything about the character's upbringing, social background, and ethnic background must be pictured in the screenwriter's mind.

The screenwriter fills many pages with this sort of information, listed in a very formal style, something between that of a police report (the factual details) and that of a psychologist's notes (the character's inner life). Most of this information is solely for the use of the screenwriter; it is the raw material from which the character is shaped. Most of it will never appear in the script, yet the character will speak and behave consistently with his or her entire background, which only the screenwriter knows.

The reader does not know, for instance, if the samurai's wife in *Rashomon* is stubborn or compliant, whether she plays the flute or writes poetry, or from what sort of family she comes. These points are irrelevant to the plot and remain undisclosed; however, they were relevant to the screenwriters while they were creating her.

In *Notorious,* the reader sees Devlin's bravery, acuity, and self-control. One also realizes that he is a romantic. Those are the characteristics needed for the film. But little is known about Devlin beyond that: nothing about his past, his family, his ambitions, his education. The screenwriters knew those details and they spent a great deal of time compiling the list.

The few traits of *Viridiana's* main character that are revealed in the script (her chastity, devotion, and humanity) are convincing and succeed in creating an impression of a living character only because they were taken from the context of the young woman's personality. Buñuel knew where those traits had originated, what factors they complemented, contrasted, and continued.

It does not matter if a script is born out of a screenwriter's interest in a certain plot or out of a fascination with an intriguing character. In both cases, the character is dependent on the plot, and the plot, in turn, is revealed through the character. The plot and the main character (or characters) enhance each other. There is dynamic unity.

The Godfather script has a huge cast of characters who originated along with and according to the basic dramatic design—the plot. Most of them are the necessary "crowd," which creates both the background and the atmosphere for the protagonist. The major characters and some of the secondary ones are directly connected to him. They not only serve to develop the protagonist's action but also reflect different aspects of his personality.

Synopsis

Don Vito Corleone's large, wood-paneled office. The Don, wearing a tuxedo, sits magisterially at his desk, while outside, his daughter Connie's extravagant wedding reception is in full swing. The Don receives petitioners. They are all here today to request favors of Don Corleone—the Godfather—"because they know that no Sicilian will refuse a request on his daughter's wedding day."[1]

Through his office window, Don Vito watches as his youngest son, Michael, and his girlfriend, Kay Adams, arrive at the reception.

Johnny Fontane, a well-known pop singer and the Don's godson, performs for the appreciative crowd. Johnny also needs a favor.

On their wedding night, Connie tries to get her bridegroom's attention. But Carlo Rizzi is too busy counting the money they have received as wedding gifts to pay much mind to her.

In his office, the Don instructs Luca Brasi, his personal bodyguard, to find out what he can about Sollozzo. Luca puts on his bulletproof vest, packs his gun, and sets off to work.

Tom Hagen, the Don's adopted son and personal *consigliere,* visits the Hollywood movie mogul Jack Woltz at his impressive estate. Woltz refuses to give Johnny Fontane the part he wants.

Sollozzo, notorious for his international heroin-trade activities, comes to meet Don Corleone. He requests the Don's financial backing and political influence for a share of his narcotics profits. Don Corleone refuses; he argues that politicians are less likely to

overlook drugs than gambling (the Don's business). Sollozzo is silently dismissed, as a bouquet of flowers arrives for the Don. They
have been sent by Johnny Fontane, who has received the lead in
Woltz's movie.

(In flashback) Jack Woltz awakens to find on his bed, in a pool
of blood, the severed head of his most cherished horse.

In a hotel room in Manhattan, Michael and Kay are planning a
simple wedding for themselves.

Don Corleone and his son Fredo are closing up the office for
the day. Paulie, the Don's bodyguard, has called in sick, so Fredo
must get the car himself. On the sidewalk, the Don stops to buy some
fruit before getting in the car. Suddenly, two gunmen appear and
shoot him down. Fredo tries to fire at the hitman, but he fumbles ner-
vously and drops his gun on the sidewalk strewn with fruit.

Michael and Kay are stunned by a newspaper headline, which
reports that Vito Corleone has been shot.

Luca Brasi goes to a nightclub. Sollozzo emerges from the
shadows. He says he would like to hire Brasi and guarantees him
fifty thousand dollars for the first shipment of narcotics that he can
deliver.

Sonny, the Don's oldest son, receives an anonymous telephone
call from a police detective who tells him that his father has been
shot. Clemenza, who heads one of the *caporegimes,* a lesser family
who provide the muscle behind the Corleones' power, arrives at the
Corleone mall to provide protection.

In the Don's office, Michael finds Sonny and Tessio, the leader
of another *caporegime,* discussing business. Sonny is ready to
wage war to avenge his father's attempted murder. Michael advises
him to wait for some word from the Don who is in a hospital.

Later that night, Tom Hagen, Sonny, Michael, Tessio, and
Clemenza try to work out a plan of action. They are worried about
Luca Brasi; they have not been able to reach him all night. A pack-
age arrives. It is a fish wrapped in Brasi's bulletproof vest. Clemenza interprets this "Sicilian message" as "Luca Brasi sleeps with
the fishes."

The hospital seems deserted when Michael arrives to visit his
father. A nurse tells him that the police ordered all the bodyguards
away. By chance, Enzo, an acquaintance indebted to the family, arrives at that time with flowers for the Don. He and Michael pretend
to patrol the hospital entrance as if they were regular guards. A police car arrives. But McCluskey, a gruff captain, orders Michael ar-
rested when he refuses to leave the premises. Michael defiantly

asks him how much Sollozzo is paying him to keep the place clear of guards. McCluskey punches him in the face, knocking him unconscious, just as Tom Hagen and Clemenza's men arrive.

During a meeting, Hagen informs Sonny and Michael that McCluskey does indeed work for Sollozzo as his personal bodyguard. Sollozzo has a new proposition: he wants the Corleones to send Michael to hear it from him. Against Tom Hagen's arguments, Sonny is desperate to get at Sollozzo. Michael agrees with his brother that this move is wise and volunteers for the job.

In the Italian restaurant, Michael and Sollozzo speak in Italian, while McCluskey devours his food. Michael demands his father's safety. Sollozzo claims that he only wants a truce. Michael asks to be excused. In the men's room, he finds the gun that Clemenza has planted behind the toilet tank. Returning to the dining room, Michael fires at Sollozzo in midsentence then immediately at McCluskey, who is still chewing. Michael drops the gun and runs out.

A series of nameless, faceless corpses appear in a car, a barber shop, an alley, an office. The five-family war is on.

Sonny goes to visit Connie and finds her bruised and crying. Carlo has obviously beaten her. Sonny is infuriated and beats his brother-in-law mercilessly when he finds him.

Kay arrives at the Corleone mall, which now resembles a battered fortress. She asks Tom about Michael's whereabouts and asks him to give Michael a letter from her, but he refuses, to avoid implicating himself.

The Don is released from the hospital under heavy police and Mafia protection. He strongly disapproves of Sonny's violent methods of handling the family's affairs. Tom Hagen tells him that Fredo is going to Las Vegas to learn the casino-gambling business; the Don nods his approval. But when Tom tells him that it was Michael who made the Corleones' big hit, the Don is terribly pained.

Connie receives a call from an anonymous woman who cancels her date with Carlo for the evening. When Connie confronts her husband with the message, he denies that he knows the girl. A fight ensues, and Carlo savagely beats his pregnant wife. In tears, Connie calls Sonny. Immediately, he drives to Connie's apartment. When he stops to pay a toll on the highway, he is surrounded by enemy cars. He dies in a hail of machine-gun fire. When the Don hears this news, he is shattered. He orders Hagen to call a meeting of the heads of the five families. "This war stops now," he declares.

The several Mafia chiefs and their aides meet to call a truce. The Don promises that there will be no more acts of vengeance unless something should happen to his youngest son, Michael.

Michael has absconded to Sicily. Escorted by his bodyguards, two young shepherds named Carlo and Fabrizio, he is on his way to Corleone, the village from which his father came. Michael spots a beautiful young girl and is instantly lovestruck. Her name is Apollonia, and she is a daughter of a café owner.

After a traditional courtship, Michael and Apollonia are married in a country wedding.

Michael is happy. He playfully tries to teach his new wife how to drive his sportscar. Don Tommasino, his host in Sicily, informs him that Sonny has been murdered. They must now hide Michael in another villa because the Corleones' enemies in Palermo could easily find and kill him. On the morning that he is to leave, Michael smiles as he watches Apollonia playing at the wheel of the car in the yard. Out of the corner of his eye, he notices his guard Fabrizio sneaking out of a side gate. As Apollonia turns on the ignition, there is an enormous explosion, which knocks Michael unconscious. Later, when he awakens, Tommasino is nursing his injuries. He learns that Apollonia has been killed.

The Godfather, much smaller and older now, is tending his vegetable garden when Michael suddenly returns. The Don expresses his hope and trust that the family, headed by Michael, can become completely legitimate.

Michael and Neri, his new and menacing bodyguard, go to Las Vegas. At the casino that his brother Fredo manages, Michael informs the owner, Moe Greene, that the Corleone family is going to buy him out. Greene is incensed. Even Fredo protests this deal. Later, Michael warns Fredo never again to "take sides with anybody against the family."

At the airport in New York, Michael is met by Kay and their small son. Kay tells him that Connie wants him to stand as godfather to Connie's son. Michael promises to consider it.

A conference is held in the Don's office. The Corleones are losing their strength in all of their districts. Tessio and Clemenza are seeking permission at least to build up their regimes if they cannot get the Don's permission to form their own families. Michael tells them to be patient and promises that, in six months, they will be able to establish themselves independently. Michael announces that Tom Hagen will be transferred to Las Vegas. The Don stands firmly by all of his son's decisions. He warns Michael that Barzini will try to arrange a meeting, using Tessio as a go-between, and that an attempt will be made to kill Michael.

Hundreds of people attend Don Corleone's funeral. Michael watches as people now fawn over Barzini, who has clearly assumed Vito Corleone's former position as the most powerful and respected underground figure in the country. Barzini finds Tessio in the crowd and tells him to arrange a meeting with Michael. Tessio talks to Michael about the meeting, as Don Corleone predicted.

Michael and Kay are standing as godparents to Connie's and Carlo's son.

Neri, dressed as a policeman, executes Barzini on a city street in broad daylight. In a motel room, three hitmen murder Tattaglia. Clemenza murders Moe Greene in a hotel elevator.

The child is christened Michael Francis Rizzi.

Michael meets Carlo at his apartment. He knows that Carlo set up Sonny's murder by luring him to Connie. Michael orders him to leave for Las Vegas to meet his wife. In the car that is to take him to the airport, Carlo is strangled by Clemenza.

Michael walks into a pizza parlor and asks for the boss. Fabrizio, the Sicilian shepherd who had betrayed him, comes out of a back room. Michael shoots him down.

At the Corleone mall, Connie is hysterical. She barges into the living room and rails at Michael for having her husband killed. Kay obviously does not believe this accusation and tries to calm her down. Connie tells Kay to read the papers to find out how many others Michael has killed. Michael coldly orders his men to remove Connie. Kay asks Michael if what Connie said is true. He stalls. He tells her that only this once will he ever allow her to ask him about his business. Again she asks, "Is it true?" After a long pause, he tells her flatly, "No." Kay is relieved. While she makes drinks, Kay watches surreptitiously as Michael receives his dutiful officers. "Don Carleone," each says reverentially as he kisses Michael's hand.

In church, Kay wears a black veil. As Mama Corleone used to, she drops many coins in the collection box, lifts a burning taper, and one by one, lights candles.

The Godfather script does not intrude on production's territory by being too specific about how the characters look, how they are dressed, or what a character's facial expression or gesture is at a particular moment.

For instance, the reader does not need to know how Kay is dressed or even what she looks like. Her last name, Adams, is enough to suggest her image — a non-Italian, non-Catholic girl, probably WASPish looking; she has to be an obvious contrast to the rest of the crowd.

The script details nothing even about Don Corleone's appearance, and the same is basically true for Michael. There is only one remark of this sort: "Apollonia is radiant as the bride; Michael is handsome despite the grotesque jaw" (the mark of the blow he took from Captain McCluskey).

Only a novice would elaborate on a character's height (unless the character's height is important to the personality or if the character is specifically a dwarf or a giant) or nose shape or shoulder width. Sometimes, however, specifics are deliberately included. For example, Connie's greedy husband, Carlo, is described as "bronzed, with curly blondish hair," "lovely dimples," and "blue eyes." Carlo's "lovely dimples" are needed to establish a certain image: a traitor with a sweet face.

Action and dialogue, not descriptions, reveal characters in a script. In *The Godfather,* the way the characters are introduced is also significant; characters often first appear in situations typical for their personalities. Don Corleone is introduced when he is receiving people in his office, meting out justice according to his own moral code. Sonny, the oldest son, is "standing impatiently by a window nearest his father, sipping a glass of wine." The young Apollonia, Michael's Sicilian bride, is first found among a group of village girls, "gathering the pink sulla, purple wisteria, and mixing them with orange and lemon blossoms. They are singing . . . as they work."

Usually, the readers of a script or the viewers of a film, eager to get to the story as soon as possible, do not pay attention to how a character is introduced. Yet they subconsciously receive the message, and they internalize the "sign" of a character: the Don's infinite might; Sonny's sensual and temperamental nature; the pastoral gaiety of the innocent Sicilian beauty.

Sometimes the screenwriter introduces a character through the eyes of another character or characters. Take for example the singer and star, Johnny Fontane. His first appearance is when Don Corleone and Tom Hagen hear him singing at Connie's wedding reception; his Italian song comes over the loudspeakers into the Don's office.

> DON CORLEONE
> What's that? It sounds like Johnny. . . .
> He came all the way from California to
> be at the wedding. . . .

You see? He is a good godson.
HAGEN
He is probably in trouble again.

This dialogue instantly reveals that Johnny may have ulterior motives for attending the wedding. Next, Johnny is singing "to the delight and excitement of the wedding guests." Michael and Kay discuss the celebrity from their place among the guests:

KAY
I didn't know your family knew
Johnny Fontane.
MICHAEL
Sure.
KAY
I used to come down to New York
whenever he sang at the Capitol
and scream my head off.
MICHAEL
He's my father's godson; he owes him
his career.

The dialogue reveals the scope of his fame: Kay "used to scream her head off" at his performances. Johnny gives the wedding its grand scale. Because of him, the extent of the Corleones' power is also introduced: Johnny owes his stardom to the Don.

Johnny Fontane is also needed to reflect an unexpected trait of the Mafia chief: the Don is idealistic, even somewhat romantic. He believes that Johnny has come to the wedding out of loyalty to the family not, as Tom Hagen suspects, because he wants a favor.

Finally, Johnny Fontane's ambition to star in a Hollywood movie allows the reader the opportunity to see some of the Corleones' methods of "getting things done." What happens to Jack Woltz—because he will not go along with the family's request, denies Fontane the role, and awakens one night in a pool of blood to find the severed head of his prized stallion in his bed—foreshadows the violence and bloodshed that will occur later in the film.

Mama Corleone is a much more important character in the script than in the film, where several scenes that included her were omitted. She represents the human and traditional aspects of the Corleone clan. Her household does not appear sinister in any way, and this normalcy makes the Mafia business seem even more unnatural for the Corleones: that they are doomed to live this way not that they do so by choice.

Mama Corleone is presented as a certain "type," with physical and behavioral traits recognizable from real-world experiences. The authors provide neither a description of Mama Corleone nor her name. She is merely Mama—an Old World Italian mother, preoccupied with her family, her kitchen, and her faith. Still, being typical does not make Mama a flat, one-dimensional character without character. The screenwriters have given her some distinctive traits within the type.

When Kay comes looking for Michael after his escape to Sicily, she tries to get Mama to forward a letter to him. At first, Mama behaves as the "type": she is concerned, hospitable, and a bit noisy, like a mother hen. But very soon her strong individual traits overpower her type:

MAMA

You're Mikey's little girl?

KAY nods yes; there are still tears in her eyes.

MAMA

You eat anything?

KAY shakes her head.

MAMA
(to HAGEN)

Disgrazia, you don't even give the
poor girl a cup of coffee?

HAGEN shrugs helplessly; on an impulse, KAY quickly moves toward MAMA, the letter extended.

KAY

Will you give this to Michael?

HAGEN

Mama, no.

MAMA

You tell me what to do? Even he don't tell
me what to do.

She takes the letter from KAY, who is grateful and relieved.

KAY

Why did they blame Michael?

MAMA

You listen to me, you go home to your family, and you find a good young man and get married. Forget about Mikey; he's no good for you, anymore.

She looks directly into KAY's eyes, and KAY understands what that means.

Before anyone else, Mama realizes that Michael's flight to Sicily is not so much a temporary escape from danger as it is an entry into the Corleone world and that for him there is no way back to Kay and to his former way of life. Mama's "forget about Mikey" foreshadows what is going to happen to Michael.

Notice that in the script there is no interaction between Mama Corleone and her husband. This separation underscores the two different aspects of the Corleones' life—home and business, being "civilians" and being "soldiers." Yet it is obvious that the Don is a family man who cares deeply about his home and his wife. After Sonny has been brutally murdered by a rival Mafia family, Don Corleone himself takes his son's body to the mortician and asks the man to do his best to repair Sonny's bullet-smashed face: "I don't want his mother to see him as he is."

Mama is a devoted wife who accepts her husband's business inasmuch as she never questions it. But when she goes through her ritual of lighting candles in church, the reader cannot help thinking that her prayers for forgiveness and mercy are on his behalf. Mama's acceptance of her husband's and sons' activities on one hand and her devotion to the Church on the other paradoxically coexist within her life, as they do within the entire universe of the film. Even the title, *The Godfather,* suggests this double meaning, being at once the name of the traditional religious role and the nickname of the Mafia chief.

In the script, religion and its events are intertwined with crime and its manifestations. Christmas coincides with the Don's shooting, and on Christmas Eve, the mall is fortified with guards. "Resurrected" from his years in exile, Michael suddenly appears before his father on Easter Sunday. More pointedly, Michael's most violent deeds, his "settling of the family's accounts," occur when Michael takes his vows as godfather to his nephew and has the child's father killed.

From the first scene of the script, Don Corleone is the mighty master, exercising his power out of tradition, honor, or friendship. He honors all requests on his daughter's wedding day. Don Corleone's petitioners believe he is the one who can "give justice." He appears not only as an all-powerful man but as a kind of spiritual authority, everybody's godfather. Only the description of his office and the word "murder," casually dropped in the dialogue, hint at the Don's underworld connection. In his office, "the blinds are closed, and so the room is dark, and with patterned shadows." In the lean style of the script, the references to "dark" and "shadows" have a prophetic ring; they become more than just descriptions of the room, they suggest the covert side of Corleone life.

The sense of the Don's power is established in a swift progression: he promises to punish two hoodlums as the court system has failed to do; he will procure citizenship for a Sicilian immigrant; he will obtain parole for another. He can easily contact Hollywood or even Congress, if necessary. Genco, his former *consigliere,* even believes that the Don can protect him from imminent death.

> GENCO is a tiny, wasted skeleton of a man. DON VITO takes his bony hand, as the others arrange themselves around his bed. . . .
> > GENCO
> Godfather, Godfather. . . . Cure me,
> You have the power. . . .
> Stay with me, Godfather. Help me meet
> death. If he sees you, he will be
> frightened and leave me in peace.

Although this is a scene of dramatic hyperbole, through Genco the reader senses the scope of the Don's power: "You can say a word, pull a few strings, eh? We'll outwit that bastard as we outwitted all of those others. (Clutching his hand) Godfather, don't betray me." Through this scene the reader also learns something of the Don's business and understands the meaning of the euphemisms "pull a few strings" and "outwit the bastards." Genco is to be believed—there have been many times in the Godfather's past when even death was frightened of him.

"The Don motions all the others to leave the room. They do. He returns his attention to Genco, holding his hand and whispering things we cannot hear, as they wait for death." Here, the Don's obvious criminality is overlooked because his code of honor is impressive. Sympathy is with Don Corleone—in Genco's hospital room, at his daughter's wedding, and ten years later as he sits gazing out into his garden. Nothing disgraceful or ignoble on his part can be seen directly. The Don has Luca Brasi, his bodyguard, execute his dirty work. (Later Michael will have Neri, his own Luca Brasi.) Even at the meetings with some of the rival leaders, he behaves humanely and justly. He is presented as a man of integrity, the ultimate family man, the godfather who guides and protects his god-children against the wickedness of the world. Even his name rings with nobility: the translation from Italian is "lionheart."

Why do the screenwriters choose not to reveal the Don's negative side? Are they trying to idealize him, or is there another purpose? Before answering this question, let us take a look at the character of Michael, the Don's youngest and favorite son. Like a fairy-tale king, Don Vito has three sons, and it is the youngest, the least likely to be his heir, who ends up "assuming the throne."

Michael Corleone is given significant buildup before he is actually introduced. The reader learns from the beginning of the script, that he is very special to his father. Don Corleone peers through the blinds in his office, awaiting his son's arrival at the wedding. When the Corleones assemble to pose for a family photograph, the Don interrupts the session: Michael has not arrived yet; "the picture will wait for him." This phrase is meaningful because not only do the Don and the family photograph put themselves on hold for Michael but it seems as though the entire plot "waits" for the protagonist to arrive.

There are, of course, many different ways in which the protagonist can be introduced. Most often he is presented immediately. But in *The Godfather*, Michael's arrival is delayed for dramatic reasons, so that the reader can first become familiar with and intrigued by his father. Through Don Corleone, the reader comes to know Michael's future and sees what he will be when he later becomes the Don.

When Michael appears at the Corleone mall, it is crowded with hundreds of guests, children, relatives, family bosses, bodyguards, and FBI agents checking cars outside the gate. Michael's Marine captain's uniform immediately sets him apart from the relatives and guests in their suits and tuxedos. He leads his girlfriend, Kay Adams, through the crowd. She, standing out more than Michael's uniform, signifies his belonging to a different circle. The year is 1945, and he has recently come home from the war. He intends to finish college; he plans to marry Kay; and he has no interest in the family's affairs. It seems that in every aspect he and the rest of the Corleones represent two opposite worlds with different values. Everything in Michael's life is open and legal: his uniform and medals and education and Kay. Michael has nothing to hide—he is clean.

In contrast to Michael, many things about the Corleones are ambiguous. They have their own understanding of justice and legality; their plans are kept secret; they talk to each other in heavily guarded privacy; even the words they use are often indirect and equivocal.

Yet Michael relishes the details of the family's history, some of which are gory, as he answers Kay's questions. For example, he tells her a story about Luca Brasi, one of the guests at the wedding. Fifteen years ago, someone wanted to take over the Corleones' olive oil business, and Al Capone sent some hitmen from Chicago to murder the Don. Luca Brasi captured the two assassins, tied them up, and then slowly chopped one of them up with an ax in front of the other. The second man suffocated—out of terror he swallowed the towel that Brasi had stuffed into his mouth. To Kay it sounds like pure fiction. The world of Al Capone and Luca Brasi does not seem completely real to Michael either: "The smile on his face seems to indicate that he is telling a tall story." He is fascinated by this idea of revenge, no matter how cruel. Otherwise, why would he relate the story to Kay, especially in such detail?

Michael is proud of his father and deeply admires his power and the reverence and fear he evokes in others. Michael is completely different from the rest of the Corleone family; he has nothing to do with their affairs, and he plans a separate life for himself. His intense inner conflict arises because he is a loving and devoted son, and he has much more in common with his father than he himself suspects. The seeds of this contradiction will grow into conflict as the plot develops. The conflict will be resolved at the end, when Michael will have come not only to join the family but to lead it.

On viewing *The Godfather* or reading the script, one would never suspect the cunning craft that went into creating the characters, especially Michael, the protagonist, the one who undergoes the most profound crisis, and the one on whom the plot most depends. He and the plot are mutually dependent: every plot twist opens a new door for Michael or closes an old one; each of Michael's actions affects the events that follow. Only through a careful analysis of the script can the real strategy of character development be perceived. Ten phases mark the changes in Michael's character.

1.) In the expository scene, Michael and the rest of his family represent two different worlds. Both are at their best: he is full of happiness, hope, and promise; they reflect festivity, generosity, and family closeness. A significant conversation between Michael and his father sums up the starting point in the development of the character.

DON CORLEONE . . . lifts his hand, and slowly touches
a particular medal on MICHAEL's uniform.

> DON CORLEONE
What was this for?
> MICHAEL
For bravery.
> DON CORLEONE
And this?
> MICHAEL
For killing a man.
> DON CORLEONE
What miracles you do for strangers.

Note the screenwriter's ironic hint: very soon Michael will perform such "miracles" for his family as well, and with just as much bravery.

> MICHAEL
> I fought for my country. It was my
> choice.
>
> DON CORLEONE
> And now, what do you choose to do?
>
> MICHAEL
> I'm going to finish school.
>
> DON CORLEONE
> Good. When you are finished, come and
> talk to me. I have hopes for you.

At this point, Michael believes that he can choose his way in life; his objectives are to complete his education and to marry Kay. His father "has hopes for him" also, which means, as the reader learns later, that Don Corleone wants to keep his son apart from his own business.

2.) There is a complication in the plot—the attempt on Don Corleone's life. After learning about it, Michael rushes to be with his family. "Michael driving during the night. There is a little fog in the air, and moisture has formed on the windshield, making it difficult to see well. . . . The Corleone mall appears before us, still decorated for Christmas. The courtyard is bathed in white floodlight, giving this place a cold and isolated look." This passage has its concrete meaning, but at the same time, it is a metaphor for Michael losing clarity and definition in his life and entering into something foreign to him, something "cold and isolated," almost eerie, chilling, frightening.

When a guard approaches Michael's car to check who he is, another guard remarks, "It's the Don's kid." At this point in the plot, Michael is not really a participant in what is going on; he is only a son who cares about his father. And because of that concern, he is now moving "toward" the Corleone mall.

3.) Still a stranger but a bit closer to the family's affairs, Michael takes on some small responsibilities. He tries to help without yet having a clear understanding of what he should do and how. He must also overcome the image of himself as a "college kid," someone, according to Sonny, who should not be "mixed up in this," otherwise "the old man'd be sore as hell." One of the descriptions shows how Michael gradually sinks into the Corleones' world: "Michael is bundled in a warm marine coat. He looks at the strange men, regarding them with an uncertain awe. They look back at him, at first suspiciously and then with the respect of his position. He is like an exile Prince. He wanders past them, and hesitates and looks at the yard."

Now the two worlds regard each other suspiciously but respectfully. Michael is not "the Don's kid" anymore. Instead, he is like "an exile Prince," the one who will ascend to the throne one day. Nothing has happened, but the atmosphere for change is set. Michael himself anticipates this change; on his last date with Kay he says goodbye meaningfully, as though he will never return.

4.) Michael's "activity," begins when he protects his father's life, nothing more. At this point, Don Vito is in the hospital.

> MICHAEL looks at the OLD MAN. His eyes are open,
> though he cannot speak, MICHAEL touches his face.
>> MICHAEL
>> Pop . . . Pop, it's me, Michael. Shhh,
>> don't try to speak. There are men
>> who are coming to try to kill you.
>> But I am with you . . . I'm with you now.

Notice the double meaning of "I'm with you now" —a very important step in Michael's gradual approach toward the Don.

This phase of the plot reveals some of the most typical of Michael's qualities: his intense spirit and his total self-control. The encounter with the police captain, who "hits Michael squarely in the jaw with all his weight and strength," is the very beginning of the conflict between the protagonist and the outside forces—the antagonistic Mafia families.

5.) In the next stage, with a dynamic development of the character and a surprising twist in the plot, Michael decides to kill Sollozzo and his guard, Captain McCluskey.

>> MICHAEL
>> Set up the meeting. . . . Sonny . . . It has to
>> be a public place . . . so I'll feel safe.
>> They'll check me when I meet them so I
>> won't be able to carry a weapon; but,
>> Clemenza, figure out a way to have one
>> planted there for me. (Pause.) Then
>> I'll kill them both.

Everyone in the room is astonished.

> SONNY
>
> You? . . .

> MICHAEL
>
> I take Sollozzo trying to kill my
> father personal, and you know I'll
> kill them Sonny.

MICHAEL radiates danger. SONNY stops laughing.

This "mutation" in the character, a dramatic twist that could not be predicted, surprises the reader as much as it does Sonny. Michael kills Sollozzo and McCluskey; he does it as a loving and devoted son, following his father's code of honor: no misdeed can go unavenged.

Michael is not following his own choices any longer. By this act of murder, he is initiated into the family.

6.) An intermission in the war between the families occurs with Michael's flight to Sicily. Now all the attention shifts to him; it is a chance to observe the protagonist closely.

The idyllic scenery in Sicily, its contrasting values, and Michael's love for Apollonia raise expectations about his escape from his father's world. Instead, Sicily only pulls Michael back, closer to the very core of the Corleones. His family name and the name of a nearby town he visits are the same. He knows that here in Corleone his grandfather was murdered, and his father, still a boy, was almost killed. Being in Sicily transforms the family stories into reality for Michael.

"A grim Sicilian village, almost devoid of people. . . . MICHAEL and his BODYGUARDS move through the empty streets of the village. They walk behind him. . . . They move down ancient steps, past an old stone fountain. MICHAEL hesitates, cups his hands, and drinks some water." Now Michael has unconsciously "baptized" himself in the water of Corleone. Soon after, the news of his brother Sonny's murder and especially the loss of Apollonia, killed by an explosion meant for him, convert Michael into a true Corleone.

There is a clash between Michael's former ideals and the reality of his existence in the present: murder, treachery, and revenge. The scenes of Michael's despair are not presented in the script—the readers themselves infer them into the story.

7.) Michael's Mafia life begins; he returns home unexpectedly on Easter morning. At the mall, the Corleone children "rush about carrying little Easter baskets, searching here and there for candy treasures and hidden Easter eggs." The Don is also outdoors, moving about in the garden.

> Suddenly he stops and looks.
> MICHAEL stands there, still holding his suitcase.
> Great emotion comes over the DON, who takes a
> few steps in MICHAEL's direction.
> MICHAEL leaves his suitcase and walks to his father,
> who embraces his favorite son.
> > DON CORLEONE
> Be my son.

This simple phrase means accept your destiny, take on your responsibilities as head of the Corleone family, defend your own and your family's dignity under all circumstances. Michael accepts. He is pained at no longer having his own choice in life. This regret is his last tribute to his former ideals.

> > MICHAEL
> From the time I was born you had laid
> this all out for me.
> > DON CORLEONE
> No, I wanted other things for you.
> > MICHAEL
> You wanted me to be your son.
> > DON CORLEONE
> Yes, but sons who would be professors,
> scientists, musicians. . . . and grandchildren
> who would be, who knows, a Governor, a
> President even.
> > MICHAEL
> Then why have I become a man like you?
> > DON CORLEONE
> You are like me. . . . I was hunted in the
> streets of Corleone when I was twelve
> years old because of who my father was.
> I had no choice.

Michael and Don Corleone, the two who were so different at the beginning of the script, start to show surprising similarity.

8.) Another step in the metamorphosis occurs. Michael is bold and ruthless now, which is his way of establishing his new position as the family head. He takes the Corleone business in his own hands and makes it clear to everyone that he, not his father, is in charge. The Godfather is now Michael's *consigliere*. He is the only person whose opinion Michael values.

> They walk through the Don's vegetable garden.
> Tomatoes, peppers, carefully tended, and covered with
> a silky netting. MICHAEL follows; the DON turns and
> looks at him. Then stoops over to right a tomato
> plant that has been pushed over. . . . MICHAEL wants to
> express something . . . hesitates.
> >   MICHAEL
> > I've always respected you.
> A long silence. The DON smiles at MICHAEL.
> >   DON CORLEONE
> > And I . . . you.

9.) At Don Corleone's funeral, Michael can see that people perceive Barzini as the one who will assume the Don's position as the most powerful Mafia figure. Now Michael's objective is to regain the strength of the Corleones and to become the Don.

As Don Vito's coffin is being lowered into the ground, Michael knows that he will get his family's power back and that others will call him Don. He has also decided to stand as godfather to his sister's baby.

10.) Michael's personal and external conflicts are being resolved while he stands as godfather to Connie's and Carlo's son and promises to protect the child against the wickedness of the world. Michael's people murder, one by one, all of his enemies and even strangle the father of the newly anointed godson. Finally, he personally avenges Apollonia's death by finding and killing his former Silician bodyguard, Fabrizio.[2]

The plot has come full circle. Michael becomes the Godfather. At the end, as at the beginning, the Don is receiving his underlings with the authority and bearing of an all-powerful leader. Kay notices people kiss Michael's hand and hears them call him "Don Corleone."

Michael Corleone is the classic example of the protagonist in a script. His internal and external conflicts are the main conflicts of the plot. The reader sees every change that takes place within the character, witnesses the total metamorphosis of his personality, and believes it. Despite his actions, Michael is sympathetic because, when first introduced, he was different. He has been gradually transformed into a Mafia chief and a pitiless Don. But the reader knows Michael's motivations, has seen the stages of the hardening of his heart, and so does not judge him harshly.

When Don Vito was a young man, establishing his position in life, he was probably very much like Michael—there are many similarities between father and son. Only over time did Don Vito earn the luxury of being human and dying peacefully in his garden, rather than dying in a shoot-out. The reader is shown only the positive aspects of Don Vito not simply because the authors wish to embellish him but because, in the plot, the Don must balance Michael's viciousness. His goodness is a redeeming promise for Michael's future. Michael will be like his father, and Don Vito in his youth was probably like Michael. They represent two different stages in the life of the same protagonist, and the title of the film, *The Godfather,* belongs to both characters.

5.
The
Construction
of
Suspense

Notorious
by Ben Hecht and Alfred Hitchcock

Notorious, 1946
   Director: Alfred Hitchcock
Screenplay: Ben Hecht
            Alfred Hitchcock

Alfred Hitchcock (1899–1980) was always accepted by both professionals and audiences. While some critics have praised him as the *auteur* and the sharp explorer of metaphysical human anxieties, others have complained about his lack of depth or concern for social issues. But no one could deny Hitchcock's technical accomplishments, visual eloquence, and infallible ability to thrill.

   Hitchcock began his career in film in 1920 as a designer of titles for Famous Players Studios in London. He had soon worked his way up to his first directorial assignment and in 1926 made *The Lodger,* his most successful film of the silent period. With the production of *Blackmail* (Britain's first synchronous sound feature) in 1929, he entered the sound era with remarkable technical mastery. Throughout the 1930s, Hitchcock built his reputation as Britain's most popular and exportable film director with such superb suspense thrillers as *The Man Who Knew Too Much, The 39 Steps, Sabotage,* and *The Lady Vanishes,* for which Hitchcock won The New York Critics Award for best director.

Hitchcock had always admired American movies and considered them technically superior to European films. So it was not a surprise when in 1937 he accepted David O. Selznick's offer to work in Hollywood. Although he was originally assigned to direct a film about the sinking of the *Titanic,* the project was almost immediately canceled. Hitchcock instead made *Rebecca,* a gothic melodrama, which won the Oscar for best picture in 1940.

During the 1940s Hitchcock firmly established his reputation as the master of suspense with such classics as *Suspicion, Shadow of a Doubt, Spellbound,* and *Notorious.* But it was in the 1950s that he had his most fruitful period. In that decade alone, he made five of his greatest films: *Strangers on a Train, Rear Window, Vertigo, North by Northwest,* and *Psycho,* not to mention the merely successful *Dial M for Murder, The Trouble with Harry,* and the remake of *The Man Who Knew Too Much.* Through the last fifteen years of his career, Hitchcock's films were much less impressive, although the director never lost his popularity. Today Hitchcock retrospectives still draw enormous crowds. When *Vertigo* and *Rear Window* were rereleased in 1983, they were two of the most successful films at the box office that year.

The Oscar-nominated screenplay for *Notorious* (1946) was written by Ben Hecht (1893–1964), one of America's most gifted and prolific screenwriters. During forty years of work in Hollywood, he wrote (alone and in collaboration) seventy screenplays and participated in work on some scripts credited to other screenwriters, among them *Gone with the Wind* and *The Foreign Correspondent.*

Notorious, according to François Truffaut, has an "exceptionally pure story line. In the sense that it gets a maximum effect from a minimum of elements, it's really a good model of scenario construction."[1] While working on the treatment and the script for *Notorious,* "Hecht and Hitchcock met several days a week from nine in the morning until six at night, Hecht either paced or lay on the floor; Hitchcock would sit primly on a straight-back chair, his hands clasped across his midriff, his round button eyes gleaming. Hecht dealt in narrative structure and development, Hitchcock in visual pyrotechnics. During the days between conferences, Hecht would type out the story-to-date, then return to Hitchcock for reconsiderations, alterations, revisions."[2] Hitchcock and Hecht used uranium hidden in fake wine bottles as the "MacGuffin" for the script (a Hitchcockian term for a secret whose discovery is important for the story). The producer was puzzled by the word *uranium.* "I said, 'This is. . . . the thing they're going to make an atom bomb with.' And he asked, 'What atom bomb?' This, you must remember, was in 1944, a year before Hiroshima," recalled Hitchcock.[3]

After having innocently researched atomic weaponry for his film, Hitchcock later discovered that he had been under FBI surveillance for three months, a fact he seemed to relish and something one could expect to happen in a Hitchcock movie.

Dramatic suspense in film is something to which people relate easily because they know from experience the feelings and emotional responses that arise during uncertain, possibly risky situations—the wish to peek ahead to see what will happen, the thrill, the anticipation of the worst, and the feverish desire for the best.

The cinema, with its unmatched ability to create the illusion of reality, has always been adept at manipulating audiences' curiosity, at making viewers completely absorbed in mysterious, dangerous, or terrifying situations. Because cinematic time is so flexible, film can condense or stretch any of those situations and, by doing so, can deepen the suspense.

The word *suspense* is often used loosely. Sometimes it can mean just captivating. Usually, the term is applied to detective stories and spy thrillers with their shoot-outs, robberies, and car chases; to all action films, whether they happen in the old West or in outer space; to slapstick or romantic comedies that are based on at least one suspenseful premise (for example, the uncertainty of whether the lovers will get together). Different degrees and kinds of suspense are built into the majority of films regardless of the genre.

Alfred Hitchcock contributed to the understanding of cinematic suspense and how it works more than any other filmmaker. He had a sophisticated knowledge of how to keep his audience worried; how to perplex his viewers; how to thwart their expectations and, at the same time, feed them new premonitions and new surprises. He knew how to make them forget all other concerns and be completely swept up by every suspenseful curve. He gave a precise definition of suspense, making a careful distinction between suspense and surprise:

> We are now having a very innocent little chat. Let us suppose that there is a bomb underneath this table between us. Nothing happens, and then all of a sudden, "Boom!" There is an explosion. The public is *surprised,* but prior to this surprise, it has seen an absolutely ordinary scene, of no special consequence. Now, let us take a *suspense* situation. The bomb is underneath the table and the public *knows* it, probably because they have seen the anarchist place it there. The public is *aware* that the bomb is going to explode at one o'clock and there is a clock in the decor. The public can see that it is a quarter to one. In these conditions this same innocuous conversation becomes fascinating because the public is participating in the scene. The audience is longing to warn the characters on the screen: "You shouldn't be talking about such trivial matters. There's a bomb beneath you and it's about to explode!"

In the first case we have given the public fifteen sounds of *surprise* at the moment of the explosion. In the second case we have provided them with fifteen minutes of *suspense*.[4]

Notorious is one of the best examples of suspense in cinema history.

Synopsis

In court, a judge sentences John Huberman to twenty years in prison for treason against the United States. After the trial, his daughter Alicia is besieged by reporters, but she refuses to speak to them. Two men secretly watch her as she makes her way out of the courthouse.

At a small gathering in Alicia's Miami Beach bungalow, most of the guests are drunk, as is the hostess. The commodore, a handsome older gentleman, keeps reminding Alicia of a cruise the two of them are to take the next day. She is more interested in a strange "party crasher," Devlin, whom she has never seen before. She sends all of her guests away, except for him, and suggests a late night drive.

Quite drunk, Alicia drives recklessly, increasing her speed to frighten her passenger. His casual mood is unchanged. The police pull the car over. This is Alicia's second offense. Devlin hands the cop his identification. The policeman apologizes, salutes, and leaves. Alicia has figured out that her guest is an agent. She is furious and orders him out of her car. He clips her in the jaw, knocking her unconscious, and takes over the wheel.

The next morning, Alicia wakes up in her bed, severely hung over and still in the clothes she was wearing the night before. Devlin is there and has already made a hangover remedy. She takes it but is still furious at him for deceiving her. He explains that he has been assigned to recruit her for intelligence work, to "smoke out" Nazis hiding in Brazil. Her father's past will make it easy for her to infiltrate this group. But she has no interest in the work whatsoever. "I don't go for patriotism . . . or patriots," she claims.[5] Devlin refutes this by playing back a recorded conversation between Alicia and her father, who is trying to persuade her to work for the Nazis. Alicia adamantly refuses. She tells her father that she hates him and what he stands for and that she loves America and would never do anything against it. Hearing the record weakens Alicia, but still she refuses to help Devlin. She tells him that she merely wants to lead her own life and have fun.

Later, on a plane over Rio de Janeiro, Devlin tells Alicia, whom he has has convinced to work with him, that he has just received news that her father has committed suicide. She feels sorry; however, now she no longer feels she has to hate him.

In Rio, Alicia and Devlin are waiting for their assignment. They are sitting in a café. Alicia has not been drinking, nor has she "met any new boyfriends," for eight days. Devlin does not give her much credit for these accomplishments. She can sense that he is attracted to her, yet he is afraid of falling in love with her.

Paul Prescott (Devlin's boss) and several American and Brazilian officials are discussing Alicia's mission. Prescott feels that she is perfect for the job that they have planned for her because "she knows how to make friends with gentlemen." Furthermore, Alex Sebastian, one of the men they are after, was a good friend of her father's and was once infatuated with her.

Devlin and Alicia have fallen in love. At Alicia's hotel, their romantic mood is interrupted by Prescott's telephone call. Devlin must go to his office.

When confronted with the plan, Devlin cannot believe that Alicia will agree to it. Beardsley, Prescott's aide, facetiously suggests that Devlin has fallen in love with Alicia. Prescott argues that Devlin is not "the sort to associate with a person of Miss Huberman's reputation." They tell Devlin that Sebastian was once in love with Alicia. Devlin leaves.

A troubled Devlin returns to the hotel. He tells her that she is to infiltrate Sebastian's life and, through him, gain access to the rest of his Nazi circle. She is quite hurt that Devlin did not protest, but she agrees to go along with the plan anyway and pours herself a drink.

The next morning in a taxi, Devlin tells Alicia that she has to remember that they met on the plane to Rio and that he is a public relations man for PanAm.

Alicia and Devlin are riding horses along a path when they see Alex Sebastian and a companion, also riding. At first, he does not notice Alicia, so Devlin sneaks a kick at her horse, sending it off wildly. Sebastian sets off to the rescue and, when he stops the horse, is quite taken with the rider.

Devlin is lonesome and worried in the café where he and Alicia had sat earlier.

In a restaurant with Sebastian, Alicia claims that she "idolized" her father and that Devlin is just someone who has been "pestering" her. Sebastian invites her to a dinner party at his house that evening.

At her hotel, Prescott tells Alicia to memorize the names of all the men that she will meet at the party.

At Sebastian's house, Mme. Sebastian, Alex's severe-looking mother introduces herself to Alicia and manages to intimidate the younger woman, however politely. She wonders why Alicia did not testify at her father's trial. Alicia quickly replies that her father asked her not to testify, for her own safety.

Sebastian enters and introduces Alicia to the other guests, four German men (including Dr. Anderson, the guest of honor) and a Brazilian couple. During dinner, Emil Hupka, one of the guests, becomes exceedingly alarmed when he notices the bottle of wine to be served. Sebastian calms him as Joseph, the butler, pours the wine.

After dinner, all of the men except Hupka discuss the seriousness of Hupka's blunder. They decide that he must be eliminated.

The next day at the racetrack, Mme. Sebastian observes, "Miss Huberman has been gone a long time." Sebastian wishes that his mother would be more cordial to his new girlfriend, but she is obviously jealous and suspicious. Meanwhile, Alicia and Devlin are trackside, pretending to have just bumped into one another. She tells him about the scientist, Dr. Anderson, and about Emil's nervousness over the wine bottle. She also tells Devlin that he "can add Sebastian to [her] list of boyfriends." She is angry at Devlin for pushing her into the situation. He reminds her that she accepted the job on her own. He feels like a fool for having ever believed that "a woman like [Alicia] could change her spots." Alicia pretends to watch the race, but she is crying behind her binoculars. Devlin reminds her that they are being watched from a distance. Sebastian's arrival breaks the conversation. Devlin leaves. Sebastian is jealous of Alicia and Devlin. She claims that she detests Devlin. Sebastian asks if she would care to prove that his rival means nothing to her.

In Prescott's office, the intelligence men are conferring. Beardsley makes a slur against Alicia's character, arousing Devlin's anger. Alicia arrives in a state of confusion: Sebastian has asked her to marry him. The men consider it a wonderfully useful opportunity.

At the Sebastian estate, Alex firmly announces to his mother (much to her chagrin) his and Alicia's wedding date.

Some weeks later, Alicia is moving into the Sebastian house. She asks Joseph for the key to a locked closet. He informs her that Mme. Sebastian keeps all the keys to the house. She coaxes Alex to get the keys from his mother. Joseph takes Alicia on a tour through the house. She notices that none of the keys fits the lock to the wine cellar. Joseph tells her that only Mr. Sebastian carries that key.

Alicia meets Devlin in the park. They decide that there must be something of great importance in the wine cellar. Devlin tells Alicia to persuade her husband to throw a party, so that he can get into the house to inspect the wine cellar himself.

Alicia finds the key to the wine cellar on Sebastian's chain and removes it.

The party is a crowded, yet elegant affair. Alicia is nervous because Devlin is late. When he does arrive, she promptly slips the key into his hand.

After slipping away from Alex, Alicia stands guard, while Devlin inspects the wine cellar. He accidentally upsets a bottle and it topples to the floor, spilling a metal ore instead of wine. Devlin scoops some of the ore into his pocket and replaces the broken bottle with an identical one.

Joseph has notified his master of a champagne shortage, and they are on their way to the cellar. Sebastian spots Alicia and Devlin in the garden together and sends Joseph away. Devlin locks Alicia in an embrace and kisses her passionately so that Sebastian can see. They pretend that Devlin was acting out of drunkenness and desperation. Devlin apologizes and leaves. Sebastian sends Alicia back to her guests.

Later in the night, Sebastian discovers that his key to the wine cellar door is missing, but in the morning the key has been returned to his chain. He also notices some disorder in the wine cellar.

Sebastian wakes his mother. In her room, he tells her that he believes he is married to an American agent and that Devlin is her accomplice.

Meanwhile, Alicia greets the new day quite relieved, believing that her husband never noticed the key missing.

Sebastian is certain that his associates will murder him (as they did Emil Hupka) when they discover the truth. Mme. Sebastian calms him. She tells him that his Nazi companions will never find out about Alicia, but he must let her mastermind his young wife's demise. "It must happen slowly," she tells him. "If she could become ill, and remain ill for a time, until. . . ." At lunch that afternoon, Alex gently persuades Alicia to drink her coffee.

In Prescott's office, Alicia is unusually sensitive to the light. Prescott informs her that the ore found in the wine bottle was uranium. Now her job is to find out where it comes from. He also tells her that he will be changing her contact; Devlin has requested a transfer to Spain.

Alicia meets Devlin in the park. He fails to mention his transfer. He notices that she looks ill. She lies and tells him that it is a hangover. Rather bitterly, she returns a scarf that he gave her, says goodbye, and staggers off.

Mme. Sebastian is pouring more coffee for Alicia. Dr. Anderson takes notice of the young woman's physical deterioration. He suggests that she see a doctor and tells her that he is going to the Carioca Mountains to do some work. He also suggests that perhaps the trip might help Alicia's condition. Alicia casually gets him to admit exactly where he is going to in the Cariocas. Alex quickly interrupts before Dr. Anderson can divulge any more information. Dr. Anderson mistakenly reaches for Alicia's cup instead of his own, alarming the Sebastians. Alicia suddenly realizes that the coffee is poisoned. She politely excuses herself and begins to make her way out of the room. Her vision is impaired and she has difficulty walking. She collapses in the hall. Dr. Anderson and the Sebastians carry her to her room against her feeble protests. Sebastian orders Joseph to have her phone disconnected.

Prescott and Devlin cannot figure out why Alicia has missed all of her meetings for five days. Devlin decides to pay a social call on the Sebastians.

Devlin arrives at the Sebastian estate when Alex is having a meeting with his associates. Joseph announces Devlin just as Dr. Anderson reports that he has been followed on several recent occasions. Sebastian is caught between the importance of Anderson's news and Devlin's arrival.

Devlin sneaks up the stairs to Alicia's room and discovers her on the verge of dying. He carries her down to his car and leaves Alex Sebastian in the hands of his Nazi conspirators.

In a government office, two secretaries are working on Alicia's file. It reports that her mission was completed successfully. One of the secretaries changes the last name on the file from Sebastian to Devlin.

The *Notorious* script includes some directions for the camera, but it is not a shooting script, with technical descriptions of every shot. *Notorious* is a readable text, almost a screenplay. The basic positions and movements of the camera are tactfully inserted into the script and only help visualize the action.

INT. SEBASTIAN'S HALL. NIGHT
FULL SHOT—The hallway is now thronged with the guests of the evening. We can see through to the drawing room; it is equally full. People are moving in and out of the buffet. Beyond the dining-room, the terrace has a number of small tables laid out. A cut shows Dr. Anderson worried and ill at ease. There is the SOUND of loud chatter and MUSIC over the whole scene. The CAMERA BEGINS TO PAN OVER until it comes ON to a BIG HEAD of Alicia. Her face wears an expression of concealed anxiety. She looks furtively toward the front door.

CLOSEUP—Her hand and handkerchief fill the screen.

Hitchcock always worked closely with his screenwriters: the dramatic and cinematic aspects of a story were inseparable to him, and he regarded the "behavior" of the camera as part of the plot. He thought out every visual detail of his film while working on the script. Hitchcock used to say that a film is ready when its script is completed—"only shooting" remains. According to him, one creates a film before shooting. To create it while standing behind the camera is similar to writing music while standing before the orchestra waiting to play it.

From the very beginning of the script, when Alicia leaves the courtroom where her father has been sentenced for treason, the camera concentrates on her.

As the people start to file out from the courtroom, CAMERA FOCUSES on a young woman, well groomed and chic. She moves forward into a CLOSEUP, her face expressionless. THE CAMERA RETREATS BEFORE HER, as she is besieged on all sides.

This close-up helps to draw the reader closer to Alicia. Hitchcock knew that the size of an image has power over the viewer's emotions, especially "when you're using that image to have the audience identify with it."[6]

Alicia is making her way through a crowd.
            VOICES
    Just a minute, Miss Huberman.
    Hold it, Miss Huberman.
    Look this way, if you please.
Flashlights explode over her face. She glances
around as more voices come across:

> VOICES
> We'd like a statement from you, Miss Huberman —
> about your father.
> For instance, do you think your father got
> what he deserved?

Miss Huberman doesn't answer. She moves forward
continuously.

> VOICES
> Could we say that you're pleased that
> your father is going to pay the penalty
> for being a German worker?

Miss Huberman passes out of scene and the CAMERA
HOLDS on two men watching after her.

> 1ST MAN
> Let us know if she tries to leave town.

The second man nods and exits.

The reader wonders why Alicia Huberman will not speak to the
reporters and wonders who the two men watching her are. The questions
draw the reader further into the script.

At the start of the next sequence, at Alicia's party, one of those
questions is answered. Alicia tells one of her guests that she is being
followed by policemen. Then, another question is immediately set up.
Alicia flirts with a man whose face cannot be seen for the entire scene.

> INT. MIAMI BUNGALOW. NIGHT (AN HOUR LATER)
> SEMI LONG SHOT — Almost filling the screen and back to camera, is
> the head and shoulders of the mysterious member of the party.
> Alicia sits opposite him, facing camera. Her head is thrown back
> and she is listening to a phonograph record. Mr. Hopkin and Ethel
> are asleep. . . . CAMERA MOVES AROUND SLOWLY until it takes in
> Alicia and her vis-à-vis in profile. For the first time we see
> Devlin's face.

This bit of script is a typical example of Hitchcockian control over
audience perception. Had the situation continued much longer, the audience would have become frustrated. The question, who is this man, would
no longer have been compelling; it would have become nagging. The
author knew exactly how long he could toy with curiosity without
alienation, how to build anticipations, satisfy them, and then suddenly
reverse them. "You keep the viewer as far as possible from what's actually
going to happen," Hitchcock said.

In *Notorious,* the romance between Alicia and Devlin is anticipated from the very beginning. Their relationship develops quickly, and in Alicia's hotel room, they exchange what has been called the "longest kiss in screen history." But now comes the dramatic twist in the plot— together, Devlin and the audience learn that Alicia's assignment is to make her way into the heart and life of Alex Sebastian. New questions lure one deeper into the story. Will Devlin deliver this message to Alicia? If so, will she accept the assignment? What does this mean for their romance, which just a short time ago seemed so perfect? The dramatic tension of the film starts to rise.

Knowing the nature of Alicia's assignment, one expects to see her efforts to get into Alex Sebastian's house, to see scenes of his seduction, and so on. Instead, there is an unexpected plot turn—a *surprise*—Alex Sebastian asks Alicia to marry him. Without the element of surprise most films would be too predictable. Surprise dismisses previously held anticipations and gives the story new lift.

Once Alicia has married Alex and infiltrated the Sebastian household, she must get the key to his well-guarded wine cellar—and here the Hitchcockian suspense starts. The more the reader identifies with the heroine, the more tense the emotions.

> INT. DRESSING ROOM. NIGHT
> MED. SHOT—Alicia moves forward to the chest on which the keys are resting. We hear the SOUND of the shower from the half-open door of the bath beyond.
> CLOSEUP—Alicia looks at the keys.

Notice that the close-up removes the barrier that separates the audience from Alicia, making her emotions more intimate. From this moment, every action, every line of dialogue in this scene serves to delay the relief of tension.

> CLOSEUP—We see her fingers sorting them through until she stops at one key. The CAMERA MOVES IN just as it did on the lock of the cellar door. The name on the key is identical. Her finger begins to hastily detach it. Over this we suddenly hear Sebastian's raised voice.

The threat that Sebastian might at any moment discover what Alicia is up to is a threat to the audience as well as to her. The audience has become an accomplice.

SEBASTIAN'S VOICE
I'm surprised at Mr. Devlin coming.
I don't blame anybody for being in
love with you. I just hope, darling,
you don't do anything tonight—to give
him any false impressions—
MED. SHOT—Alicia is rooted for the moment. She gets
the key and crosses to the center of the room. She
now has the key in her possession. She looks down at
it in her open palm.

Anticipation is stretched more and more. While Alicia is wondering where to hide the key, Sebastian's voice tells her cheerfully that he is coming (the danger is reinforced), and he asks Alicia not to "get impatient" while waiting for him. In light of what is happening, the irony of these phrases only underlines the gravity of the situation. The audience is glad that Alex Sebastian does not realize what is going on and even more afraid of what will happen when he does.

The camera pans Sebastian into the bedroom. Now the camera itself stretches out the time, and there is another delay. What will happen with the key? Sebastian talks at length about his love for Alicia and about his trust in her. Here is yet another twist to make the situation more tense and to remind Alicia and the audience that the more he loves her and trusts her the stronger will be his reaction when he discovers the truth.

The authors continue to increase the suspense:

CLOSEUP—Sebastian taking her clenched hands in his.
MED. SHOT—Sebastian and Alicia. He opens one hand to kiss it,
but before he can open the other, which contains the key, Alicia
slips her arms around his neck. He kisses her.
CLOSEUP—Alicia. We see her right hand lower itself behind his
back. She opens it and drops the key onto the soft carpet.

The audience breathes a sigh of relief, but the authors take full advantage of the challenge they put to Alicia. Even after she has dropped the key from her hand, she still must get it out of Alex's range of vision.

CLOSEUP—Alicia. In her embrace, slowly turns Sebastian away as
though in a kind of ecstatic sway.
CLOSEUP—Alicia. Her feet approach the key. She kicks it just under the bureau.

The danger has passed for the time being. The expectation that Sebastian will be deceived is fulfilled for the present.

> CLOSEUP—Key, resting almost out of sight underneath the bureau.

Analyzing this scene, one can see that stretching out the dangerous moment has made it particularly suspenseful and cinematic.

As Hitchcock stated quite clearly in his example of the bomb underneath the table, suspense and time are interrelated. Classic Hitchcockian suspense nearly always concentrates on a race against time. Whenever the audience is aware of a clock ticking, the sense of danger is increased and the suspense is therefore intensified. The "ticking" need not necessarily come from a clock. In *Notorious,* there is an episode in which the sense of time running out comes not only from the butler, who is about to go down to the wine cellar, but also from the bottles, whose number is ever diminishing. In these scenes, a new wave of suspense takes the tension to a higher pitch.

Holding the key that Alicia has passed to him, Devlin waits for her so they can go to the wine cellar. But Alicia, fearful of arousing suspicion, cannot leave Alex and the guests too suddenly.

> MED. SHOT—Alicia is sipping some champagne. She glances down behind the buffet.
> CLOSEUP—a group of eight bottles of unopened champagne.

Alicia is told by Joseph that he will need more champagne soon: "Madame, we seem to have a number of very thirsty guests." The "clock" has been set.

On his way to the cellar, Devlin stops at the bar. He sees that there are now only four bottles of champagne. The butler's "hand comes in and takes one, leaving only three." Now the "clock" is ticking.

> INT. HALLWAY. NIGHT
> MED. SHOT—Alicia with Sebastian and a group of people around them. Conversation is general. . . . A footman arrives with a tray of drinks. There is a general exchange of glasses.

The glasses are another persistent reminder of the time element.

> CLOSEUP—FROM Alicia's VIEWPOINT—the laden tray with hands exchanging empty glasses for full ones.

Now the camera itself emphasizes that the wine is running out.

While Devlin investigates the wine cellar, Alicia stands guard at the door. The party continues:

> INT. DINING ROOM. NIGHT
> MED. SHOT—Joseph, serving at the buffet. He glances down at the wine. With his finger he counts out the remaining number: three.

The butler is no longer figuring out *if* he should go to the cellar but *when* he should go. Meanwhile, Alicia is alarmed by the sound of glass breaking in the cellar. She joins Devlin, who has discovered the uranium in the broken bottle.

There is a collision between Alicia's fear that the noise could be heard upstairs and her relief that Devlin has found what they were looking for. The audience shares her fear and her relief. But the suspense continues—they must now cover their tracks.

> INT. DINING ROOM. NIGHT
> MED. SHOT—Joseph still serving at the buffet, now looks down. There is only one bottle of wine left. He thinks for a moment and then begins to look for Mr. Sebastian.

Again, anticipation is prolonged.

> INT. WINE CELLAR. NIGHT
> MED. SHOT—Devlin is pushing the pieces of glass underneath the bottom shelf. He is scooping sand into a small pile.

Notice that the authors chose this point to reestablish the shortage of champagne, immediately before Devlin and Alicia must clean up. Each reminder of the time element increases the tension.

> INT. HALLWAY. NIGHT
> MED. SHOT—We see Joseph crossing to Sebastian.
> CAMERA MOVES IN until we have the two together.
>> JOSEPH
> I'm afraid we shall need some
> more champagne.
>> SEBASTIAN
> Really? I thought we had
> provided enough. I'd better
> go down with you then.

Sebastian turns to guests and we half hear him excuse himself. He moves away with Joseph.

The action moves closer to the "bomb explosion." In Hitchcockian suspense, the audience is provided information that the characters of the film do not have. They, for example, know that Joseph and his master have started for the cellar—Alicia and Devlin do not. With bated breath the audience tries to figure out at which moment Alex and Joseph will reach the cellar.

INT. CELLAR. NIGHT
MED. SHOT—Devlin is finishing off the bottle. The CAMERA MOVES IN until only the neck of the bottle fills the screen. He is putting on the tinfoil cap and squeezing it tightly between his fingers.

Because the screenwriters now depict actions that coincide in time, there is an agony of suspense that increases steadily as Alex and Joseph near the cellar. The audience expects Devlin to manage the operation well but is fearful and anxious that he may fail.

MED. SHOT—With a grunt of satisfaction [Devlin] puts the bottle on the shelf among the others. The CAMERA PULLS BACK as Devlin steps down and with his handkerchief gives a few final swishes to the floor. The CAMERA PANS them both over to the door.
INT. CORRIDOR. NIGHT
MED. SHOT—As they both emerge and the door is closed with a click, Devlin hands Alicia back the key.

The suspense surrounding the wine cellar is over. But the audience's tension is relieved only for a moment: as Alicia and Devlin turn into the main corridor, they hear footsteps. Alicia, as does the audience, sees Sebastian and Joseph coming down. She hurries Devlin through the glass door. Sebastian sees them. He sends Joseph away, so that he will not be a witness to this embarrassing scene.

Notice how unpredictable is the action in the following episode:

CLOSEUP—Devlin and Alicia, outside glass door.
She grabs him and whispers:
ALICIA
Wait—there's someone . . .

> DEVLIN
> (whispering)
> I'm going to kiss you—
> ALICIA
> No, he'll think we're—
> DEVLIN
> That's what I want him to think.
> He embraces her; they kiss. Slowly, the kiss which
> has started merely as a trick to fool Sebastian,
> turns into the real thing for both of them. . . .
> DEVLIN
> (whispering)
> Push me away—

He asks Alicia to act as if they were caught.

The thrill of the wine cellar scene—the emotional experience that the audience has gone through with this couple—has made the audience a devoted accomplice. Now, being closer to them, viewers are more prepared to empathize with Alicia's and Devlin's situation: Sebastian, their mutual adversary and an enemy of their country, has marital rights to Alicia; they have to tolerate his sarcasm and his jealousy; she has to explain herself to him; what's more, Devlin must tell him something that is necessary at the moment but that, at the same time, is, paradoxically, a very personal, painful truth.

> SEBASTIAN
> I'm sorry to intrude—on this
> tender scene—but mother saw
> you come this way.
> ALICIA
> Alex—not here. We'll talk
> alone.
> SEBASTIAN
> You are afraid to speak in
> front of him?
> ALICIA
> No. I couldn't help what
> happened. He's been drinking.
> SEBASTIAN
> (sarcastically)
> He carried you down here—?

> ALICIA
>
> Alex—please!
>
> SEBASTIAN
>
> You love him.
>
> ALICIA
>
> No. Absolutely—no.
> (to Devlin)
> Please go!
>
> DEVLIN
>
> For what it's worth—as an
> apology—she's telling the truth.
> I knew her before you—loved her
> before you—but wasn't as lucky
> as you. Sorry, Alicia.

Alicia tries to convince Alex that she could not stop Devlin from kissing her because he was drunk and that she did not want to make a scene. Sebastian appears ready to believe her, and he asks her to go upstairs and join their guests.

It would seem that things are calming down, that the danger has passed, but suddenly Sebastian remembers the champagne and summons Joseph to go to the wine cellar with him.

> CLOSE SHOT—Sebastian puts his hand in his pocket and pulls out the keys.
> CLOSEUP—His fingers run through the keys searching for the right one.
> BIG HEAD. Sebastian is looking down. His expression changes.

He tells Joseph that champagne is not necessary—they have plenty of whiskey and wine. Joseph agrees. They leave, but the camera stays on the wine cellar door. Here, the camera itself takes on the role of a sarcastic observer: Sebastian does not have the key to open the door.

Although in *Notorious* the suspense is focused on the key and on the fake wine bottle that contains uranium, it is not these scenes that are the climax of the film.

Hitchcock has emphasized many times that it is wrong to attach too much dramatic importance to the uranium in *Notorious*. This specific "MacGuffin" could be changed. It could be industrial diamonds instead, or something else. Because "*Notorious* was simply the story of a man in love with a girl who, in the course of her official duties, had to go to bed with another man and even had to marry him. That's the story."

The conflict in *Notorious* is not only between the FBI agents, who are trying to discover what is going on at the Sebastians', and the Sebastians, who are trying to hide it, it is also, and most importantly, between love and duty; it is Alicia's and Devlin's conflict. Thus, the climax in *Notorious* is not when Devlin finds the uranium but when he rescues Alicia from the Sebastians and asks her to be his wife.

After Alex discovers that Alicia is a spy, he and his mother slowly poison her. Devlin wonders what has happened and why Alicia has not been in contact with his office. Thinking about his impending transfer, but reluctant to leave without seeing her, he goes to the Sebastians' home.

While Alex is busy with his "business associates," Devlin makes his way to Alicia's room; there he finds her nearly dead.

> ALICIA
> They are poisoning me—slowly.
> . . . Alex and his mother. They
> found out. (Sinks back exhausted)
> DEVLIN
> (starts lifting her up)
> Alicia, come on—get up! We've
> got to get you out of here.
> ALICIA
> (opens eyes again—foggily)
> I thought you'd gone away to Spain.
> DEVLIN
> (propping her up—looking around
> for a robe)
> I had to see you and speak my piece
> once. I was getting out because I
> love you. I couldn't bear you and
> him together. . . .
> (starts putting robe around
> her shoulders)
> Try to sit up, Alicia.
> ALICIA
> (trying to sit on edge of bed)
> You love me—Oh, Dev, if you'd
> only said it before!

Here begins the resolution of the film's conflict—love versus duty—and the step toward the culmination of the action—the climax.

From the fragmented, barely audible phrases Alicia is able to utter, Devlin finds out that Alex and his mother are hiding her "illness"; moreover, they are also hiding everything else they know about her. "They would kill Alex—if they knew."

Alicia cannot walk:

> ALICIA
> Can't. You go—alone. Thanks.
> Hurry, Dev. They're all in the house.
>> DEVLIN
> Unh—unh. You're never getting rid
> of me.
>> ALICIA
>> (weakly)
> Never tried to.
>> DEVLIN
> I'm going to crawl after you on my
> hands and knees for the rest of my
> life. And I'm beginning right now.

Although the danger has by no means passed, this scene is the climax of the love story in which, as Hitchcock said, "a man is in love with a girl who, in the course of her official duties, had to go to bed with another man." Now, as far as the lovers are concerned, only the two of them matter, and even if the Nazis were to kill them now, this romance would still have ended with the lovers united. In the conflict of love versus duty, love has been victorious.

However, one obstacle remains—the secondary conflict in *Notorious,* between the government agents and the Nazi group.

> SEBASTIAN
> (approaching them on the steps)
> Alicia—what are you doing?
> What is this, Mr. Devlin?
>> DEVLIN
> I'm taking her to a hospital—
> to get the poison out of her.
>> SEBASTIAN
> Poison?
>> DEVLIN
> Everybody knows—except your
> friends downstairs—

Devlin challenges Alex to tell his friends who Alicia is; he promises to keep his "mouth shut. So will the department."

> DEVLIN
> (whispering to Sebastian)
> Is it a deal—or do we start shooting?

The tension of this scene depends entirely on the unpredictability of Sebastian's behavior: which force is stronger in him, the will to live or the desire to see Alicia and Devlin punished, even killed?

There is no clock ticking in this scene (although, perhaps the "business associates," who may at any moment burst upon the scene, are analogous to the ticking clock); there is no hidden bomb; the audience knows no more than do the protagonists. In other words, there is no real suspense in the master's classic definition. But this scene is of such emotional intensity that it is difficult not to describe it as "full of suspense." It is the confrontation between the two opposing parties, and soon the outcome of this clash will show who wins and who loses.

Now there is another step toward the resolution—Mme. Sebastian appears from her room.

> SEBASTIAN
> I'm taking her back to her room.
> DEVLIN
> It'll raise quite a rumpus if you try.
> MME. SEBASTIAN
> Alex—wait. He knows?
> SEBASTIAN
> Yes.

Two of the Sebastians' associates enter the hall downstairs.

> MME. SEBASTIAN
> (whispering)
> Help him, Alex.
> DEVLIN
> I'm glad you've got a head on you,
> Madame.

An unexpected twist—Alex and his mother are forced to become partners with Alicia and Devlin. When Sebastians' associates start asking what happened to Alicia, he helps Devlin to support her on the stairs—indeed, this act is his defeat, he gives in. Devlin and Alicia prevail as Sebastian's associates watch from below.

SEBASTIAN
(sweating, his voice slow)
She collapsed. Mr. Devlin heard
her scream—while he was waiting
for me—

DEVLIN
Yes—I called the hospital—as
soon as I saw how she was—

MME. SEBASTIAN
You have a car, Mr. Devlin?

DEVLIN
Yes, in front.

MME. SEBASTIAN
Your hat, Alex.

MATHIS
You are going with them, Madame?

MME. SEBASTIAN
No, Alex will call me up—I'll wait here.

Devlin, Sebastian, and Alicia reach the door. One of Alex's associates opens it for them, and the three move down the outside steps to the car. It would appear that all is well. But there is another brief delay—Alicia is about to faint.

ALICIA
Hurry up—I'm dizzy—the air—

DEVLIN
Take deep breaths.
He helps Alicia into the car. The group is watching
from the open doorway.

SEBASTIAN
Just a minute. I must sit next
to her.

DEVLIN
(climbing into car)
No room, Sebastian.

SEBASTIAN
(wildly and tensely)
You must take me! They're watching.

DEVLIN
(throwing the car in gear)
That's your headache, partner.

SEBASTIAN
(breaking)
No—no—no. Take me—no—no—!
The car shoots off. Sebastian stands a minute, defeated,
then slowly turns back toward the house.

The two suspense scenes, which focus on the key and on the wine cellar, are not directly related either to the Alicia-Devlin conflict or to their confrontation with the Sebastians, but these scenes touch the very nerve of the story. They carry the action forward; they charge the screen with emotion and energy; they serve to bridge the distance between the characters and the audience. As scenes of great tension, they reveal much about the personalities of Alicia and Devlin. Their true natures are seen at these sharp moments.

Not everything called *suspense* conforms to Hitchcock's formula. One can think of many suspenseful scenes in which neither the viewers nor the characters know where the dangers are hidden or when they might strike. Yet, the image of the ticking clock and hidden bomb, better than anything else, helps us to understand the nature of suspense.

6.
Transforming Literature into Cinematic Space and Time

Rashomon
by Akira Kurosawa and
Shinobu Hashimoto

Rashomon, 1950
  Director: Akira Kurosawa
Screenplay: Akira Kurosawa
            Shinobu Hashimoto

Akira Kurosawa (b. 1910) is the most influential Japanese director in the
West, his films often having been openly imitated by directors in America and
Europe. *Yojimbo* was remade in Italy as the classic spaghetti western, *A Fistful
of Dollars.* In Hollywood, *The Seven Samurai* was remade as *The Magnificent
Seven,* and *Rashomon* as *The Outrage.* Kurosawa is often seen as a cultural
link between the East and the West. His interest in Western culture was
evident at an early age when he studied Western painting techniques in art
school. He loves European literature and has made free adaptations of

William Shakespeare's *Macbeth* and *King Lear* (as *Throne of Blood* and *Ran*, respectively), Fyodor Dostoyevsky's *Idiot,* and Maksim Gorky's *Lower Depths.*

Seven years after Kurosawa directed his first film (*Judo Saga,* 1943), he made *Rashomon,* for which premieres were held in Tokyo on 25 August 1950 and in New York on 26 December 1951. *Rashomon* was the first masterpiece of Japanese cinema to receive international recognition. When it was shown at the Venice Film Festival in 1951, it took the Golden Lion and virtually introduced Japanese cinema to Western audiences. The following year, the film won the Academy Award for Best Foreign Film. *"Rashomon* became the gateway for my entry into the international film world," wrote Kurosawa.[1]

In one of the earliest American reviews of the film, Richard Griffith wrote, "Whoever Akira Kurosawa is, however he came into his greatness as a film director, it was by more than knowing his lenses and his cameras. He knows how difficult it is to live, how necessary to love."[2]

The script for *Rashomon* was written by Kurosawa with Shinobu Hashimoto, a screenwriter and producer. In his memoirs, Kurosawa recalled how they worked together and how they met. "Hashimoto had visited my home, and I talked with him for hours. He seemed to have substance, and I took a liking to him. He later wrote the screenplays for *Ikiru* (1952) and *Seven Samurai* (1954) with me." The script for *Rashomon* was based on two short stories by Ryūnosuke Akutagawa (1892–1927), "In a Grove" and "The Rasho Gate," which is more often translated as "Rashomon." "The script was done as straightforwardly and briefly as possible," wrote Kurosawa.

It was more than a year before the Daiei Studio bought the script; they were still harboring many doubts. "It turned out that they found the script baffling and wanted me to explain it to them. 'Please, read it again more carefully,' I told them. 'If you read it diligently, you should be able to understand it.'" Kurosawa has called the film "a strange picture scroll that is unrolled and displayed on the ego." With its exquisitely sparse and highly organized visual compositions, the film does indeed resemble ancient scroll paintings. A certain contribution to the film's aesthetic quality was made by Kurosawa's cameraman, Kazuo Miyagawa, one of the best Japanese cinematographers. They actually filmed the sun. "These days [the late 1980s] it is not uncommon to point the camera directly at the sun, but at the time *Rashomon* was being made, it was still one of the taboos of cinematography," said Kurosawa.

Akira Kurosawa often edits and writes, or at least cowrites, all of his films. He devotes his attention to the dramatic and literary quality of scripts. "With a bad script even a good director cannot possibly make a good film," Kurosawa wrote. He sees his own screenwriting as an integral part of creating films, insisting that "the root of any film project for me is [an] inner need to express something. What nurtures this root and makes it grow into a tree is the script. What makes the tree bear flowers and fruit is the directing."

Over the years, Kurosawa has exhibited an impressive range of styles, from the bold realism of *Ikiru* to the lyricism of *Rashomon,* to the epic adventure of *The Seven Samurai,* to the monumental baroque of his recent film *Ran.* Unlike many other directors, Kurosawa has always adapted his style to the story rather than the story to his style. The sense of the director in a Kurosawa film is evident not so much in recurring themes as in the incomparable significance and virtuosity of his visual language.

When adapting a novel or a short story into a screenplay, the screenwriter acts as an intermediary between the illusive, internal world of literature and the external, physical world of film. Like an author, the screenwriter uses words, but like the filmmaker, thinks in visual images; each word has to be "seen" by the reader.

In script text, there can be no author digressions, meditations about characters or situations, or even descriptions of a character's thoughts or feelings: "The police agent is proudly testifying. Beside him, tied up, sits the bandit, Tajomaru. Behind them sit the woodcutter and the priest."[3] It is the opposite of what can be seen in this passage from a short story: "His mind, after making the same detour time and again, came finally to the conclusion that he would be a thief. But doubts returned many times. Though determined that he had no choice, he was still unable to muster enough courage to justify the conclusion that he must become a thief."[4]

Everything that the screenwriter wants to say about the characters and their inner lives can be expressed only through what they do and what they say. "Something that you should take a particular notice of is the fact that the best scripts have very few explanatory passages," writes Kurosawa in his memoirs. "It's easy to explain the psychological state of a character at a particular moment, but it's very difficult to describe it through the delicate nuances of action and dialogue."

Unlike literary text, which is usually written in the past tense (the writer is recounting a past event, and from time to time evaluating it), everything in script text is written in the present tense. Even flashbacks are presented as if they are occurring right now. One can argue that viewers never forget that flashbacks *are* the past, which is true. But flashbacks appear to unfold in the present because the viewers are taken into the past to watch the action "as it happens," as in the following piece:

PRIEST
Yes, sir. I saw the murdered man when
he was still alive. Well, it was about
three days ago. It was in the afternoon.
Yes, it was on the road between Sekiyama
and Yamashina.
The priest is walking along a road that winds through
a bamboo grove. From the opposite direction a samurai
approaches, leading a horse by the bridle. On the
horse is a woman, sitting sidesaddle. The priest
steps back and looks after them; they recede into
the distance.
PRIEST (off screen)
Her hat had a veil. I couldn't see her face.[5]

The adaptation can be dependent on its literary source, translating almost every episode into the script, or it can be loose and elliptical. In any case, the screenwriter usually retains the main line of the plot and the causal connections between events in the work being adapted. For instance, when turning Mario Puzo's novel *The Godfather* into a script, Coppola and Puzo eliminated some characters and a number of episodes, but they did not change the cause-and-effect relationships of the events. (Michael had to hide in Sicily because he killed Sollozzo, and he did that because his enemies tried to assassinate his father.) Any change in the causal succession would transform the whole narrative into something completely different and unrecognizable.

Screenwriters can, however, freely change the temporal succession of events without altering the content of the literary original. The screenwriter can start the script from the end of a novel or story and flashback to the beginning, or start in the middle and move in either direction, or do both by crosscutting the flashbacks with the flashforwards.

The screenwriter has incomparable flexibility in dealing with space and time. Time can be compressed or stretched. At any moment, the flow of events can be interrupted or reversed. Action can be frozen, or an episode can be repeated over and over again; for instance, an incident can be shown at one time in reality and at another time as a character's recollection.

In film, time is inseparable from space. In literature, they can be separate, and the spatial aspect may be excluded from the narrative entirely. In a short story in which a character is writing a letter, the author's focus might only be on the character's psychological experience not on where it takes place. In a film, this character must be placed somewhere—a room, a library (unless it is an experimental film and the director has the character surrounded by only the white flatness of the screen).

In adaptation, the screenwriter makes incompletely defined literary space concrete. The location and its specific physical and spiritual qualities are of the utmost importance, and they are introduced before anything else.

Akira Kurosawa and Shinobu Hashimoto based their script on two of Ryūnosuke Akutagawa's short stories, "In a Grove" and "The Rasho Gate." This adaptation is faithful to the original in terms of atmosphere, main characters, and basic events, but the screenwriters have shaped their own plot out of the literary material and presented their own point of view on the characters' actions and on human nature in general. Their major device in accomplishing this shift was the entire restructuring of the space and time of the literary source.

Synopsis

Under the Rashomon, the half-ruined gate of twelfth-century Kyoto, a Buddhist priest and a woodcutter take shelter from a rainstorm. They are shocked by an event that has recently occurred. The priest says that there has never been anything "as terrible as this."[6] The woodcutter recounts the story to a commoner who has also sought refuge from the pouring rain. "It was three days ago," begins the woodcutter. "I'd gone into the mountains for wood . . ."

The woodcutter walks through the woods. His ax glints in the sunlight. He stops in surprise when he notices a woman's reed hat and veil hanging from a branch and several other small items scattered nearby. Suddenly, the woodcutter draws back in horror as he notices a corpse. In a panic, he runs away, dropping his ax.

The woodcutter, kneeling in a prison courtyard, testifies to an unseen judge: yes, he was the first person to find the dead body. He lists the articles he discovered and swears that he has left nothing out.

The priest testifies in the same court. He says that three days prior he had seen the murdered man while he was still alive . . .

The priest walks through the woods. From the opposite direction comes a samurai leading a horse by the bridle. On the horse rides a woman.

Back in the courtyard, the priest claims that he could not see the woman's face through her veil and that the man had a sword, a bow, and arrows.

A police agent testifies. Beside him sits Tajomaru, the bandit, tied up. The police agent says to the unseen judge that, when he caught Tajomaru, the bandit was carrying a Korean sword, a bow, and arrows and that he had been thrown by a horse. With emphatic pride, Tajomaru states that he killed the samurai three days ago . . .

In the woods, Tajomaru is sleeping under a huge tree. The samurai and the woman on the horse pass him. Tajomaru opens his eyes. A breeze blows aside the woman's veil. "I thought I had seen an angel. And right then I decided I would take her." Tajomaru approaches the samurai and tells him that in the grove he keeps antique swords, daggers, and mirrors, which he is willing to sell cheaply. They leave together, and the woman remains alone on the road.

As the samurai nears the grove, Tajomaru suddenly draws his sword and attacks him. They fight; the samurai loses. Tajomaru ties him to a tree and triumphantly tears through the woods to the woman. He tells her that her husband has been bitten by a snake. "The sight of her made me jealous of that man; I started to hate him. I wanted to show her what he looked like all tied up." Tajomaru runs back to the grove, pulling the woman along by the wrist. When she sees her husband, she attacks the bandit with her dagger, misses, and attacks him again. "She fought like a cat." But eventually, she succumbs to Tajomaru, giving herself to him.

When the bandit gets up and is ready to leave the grove, the woman runs after him. She says that either the bandit or her husband must die; she wants to belong to whichever one kills the other. The bandit cuts the rope that binds the samurai and gives him back his sword. They cross swords again and again, "over twenty-three times. No one had ever crossed over twenty with me before. Then I killed him," says Tajomaru.

The woman runs away. Tajomaru cannot find her. He takes the horse and the man's sword but forgets the woman's dagger. "That was the biggest mistake I ever made."

At the gate, the rain continues to pour. The priest tells the commoner that he saw the woman in the prison courtyard and that she was not at all as willful as Tajomaru has described her. On the contrary, she was rather miserable and meek.

In the courtyard, the woman testifies. She says tearfully that, after having taken advantage of her, the bandit sneered at her husband, took the samurai's sword, and left . . .

The woman rushes to her husband. She lies crying at his feet. The samurai looks at her coldly and cynically, despising her. Cutting the rope with her dagger she asks him to kill her but not to look upon her with hatred. She cries and begs; it does not help. In total despair she raises the dagger above the samurai.

In the courtyard, she says that at that moment she fainted, and when she opened her eyes, the dagger was in her husband's chest.

The rain keeps on as the three men huddle under the Rashomon. The story confuses the commoner. The priest informs him that there is also the husband's account of the murder, which was related through a medium.

The medium, a woman, danced madly in the wind. In the background are the priest and the woodcutter. Through her mouth comes the voice of the dead samurai. "The bandit, after attacking my wife, . . . tried to console her. . . ."

In the grove, Tajomaru asks the woman to go with him because he loves her. She wants him to kill her husband first. Her words shock the bandit. He throws her to the ground and holds her down with his foot. He asks the husband what to do with her. Kill her? Spare her? "For these words I almost forgave the bandit," says the samurai. The woman manages to free herself and flees into the woods. Tajomaru tries but cannot catch her. He returns to the samurai, cuts the ropes that bind him, and leaves.

The samurai is weeping. He notices the woman's dagger on the ground, takes it, raises it high above his head, and thrusts it into his chest. "I lay quietly in this stillness. . . . Then someone's hand grasped the dagger and drew it out."

Under the Rashomon, the woodcutter protests; there was no dagger when he found the corpse. The samurai was killed by a sword, he insists. The commoner accuses the woodcutter of having viewed the entire scene and not having testified about it. The woodcutter explains that he simply did not want to get involved with the police; but now he will tell the truth . . .

In the grove, the woman cuts the rope that binds her husband and falls to the ground sobbing between the samurai and the bandit. Tajomaru begs her to go with him. If she agrees, he will marry her, do anything she wishes, even give up being a bandit. The woman says that it is not for her to decide; only men must make such decisions. The bandit reaches for his sword, but the samurai refuses to risk his life for the "shameless whore." He is surprised that she does not kill herself. He offers the woman to the bandit, but now Tajomaru also looks upon her with suspicion. He is ready to leave and does not want her to follow him. The woman breaks down in tears. The samurai berates her for crying, but Tajomaru comes to her defense: "Women cannot help crying. They are naturally weak." Now the woman breaks into hysterical laughter. She accuses both men of being weak and cowardly for refusing to fight for her. "A woman can only be won by the strength of the sword." The men reluctantly begin their awkward duel. After many passes, the bandit corners the samurai. The samurai cries and pleads for his life, but Tajomaru raises his sword and kills him. Meanwhile, the woman flees into the woods. Tajomaru runs after her but trips and falls. He is dirty, exhausted, and somewhat crazed.

The rain does not stop. Under the Rashomon, the commoner questions the accuracy of the woodcutter's story. The woodcutter claims that he never tells lies. The priest complains that he is pained that men do not trust each other. Suddenly, they hear a baby cry. The commoner runs to the rear of the gate and there finds an abandoned infant. He kneels over it and removes its clothes. The priest and the woodcutter are amazed by his actions. The priest takes the baby away from him. The woodcutter accuses the commoner of being selfish and evil. The commoner, in turn, accuses the woodcutter of the same. He has figured out that it was the woodcutter who stole the woman's valuable dagger, which was missing from the scene of the crime. By his silence, the woodcutter admits his guilt. He is visibly ashamed. The priest looks on disapprovingly as the commoner laughs and leaves in the rain.

The rain trickles to a stop. The woodcutter tries to take the infant from the priest, but the other resists, thinking that the woodcutter only intends to steal what little clothing is left. The woodcutter denies the charge with heartfelt humility. "I have six children of my own," he tells the priest. "One more wouldn't make it any more difficult." The woodcutter takes the baby. The priest apologizes for not having trusted him. With the baby in his arms, the woodcutter leaves the Rashomon.

In the script, the bandit, the woman, and the samurai all plead guilty, and the reader is convinced by their testimonies. At least two of the characters are lying, possibly all three, if some other person killed the samurai. However, none of them lies to escape punishment: *Rashomon* is not a detective film.

The basic plot of the script is close to that of Akutagawa's short story "In a Grove"—the same rape and murder; the same triangle of the samurai, his wife, and the bandit; the same conflicting claims of each being the killer. The short story consists of the testimonies and confessions of seven characters; seven monologues follow each other: the woodcutter testifies, then the traveling Buddhist priest, the police agent, the woman's mother, the bandit, the woman, and finally the dead samurai.

The script contains deviations from "In a Grove"; some are less, others more, significant. For example, in the script, the woman's mother is omitted. In the story, she testified that they were a good couple; that the samurai would never "provoke or antagonize another person"; and that her "spirited, lovely girl" was always pure and faithful.[7] This information and this personage were not needed for the plot and were therefore excluded from the script.

In "In a Grove," the samurai's wife confesses that she "stabbed the small sword through the lilac-colored kimono into his breast." In the script, she stabs the samurai almost unconsciously, which makes the plot more ambiguous.

In the short story, the bandit gagged the samurai with bamboo leaves to prevent him from calling out. In the script, this detail is omitted— visually, this scene would have been too vulgar and naturalistic. It would not have fit the film stylistically.

In the story, the woodcutter found only a rope and a comb at the foot of the tree. In the script, he finds "a woman's reed hat with a veil, dangling on a branch near the ground," a bit farther a man's hat, then a piece of rope, and after that an amulet case. The reason for the additions is clear: each new item raises more interest and more suspense. All of these items taken together constitute a telling still life in which every piece suggests something about its owner.

There are other minor additions and omissions in the script, but what most drastically changed the plot was the introduction of a new character—the commoner. He appears in the beginning of the film as if carried in by the storm, "splashing through puddles," his head covered with a rag; at the end he disappears back into the pouring rain.

The commoner is an outsider, the only one of the eight characters in Kurosawa's *Rashomon* who has no connection to the events in the grove. Noticing that the priest and the woodcutter are shocked by something, he wants to amuse himself with hearing their story while he waits out the rainstorm. Because of him, the priest and the woodcutter are prompted to collect their thoughts. The commoner forces the woodcutter to tell what he really witnessed in the grove and figures out that the woodcutter stole the dagger. He also finds an explanation for the lies: "Well, men are only men . . . everyone wants to forget unpleasant things, so they make up stories." He himself does not mind a lie, if it is an interesting lie.

When the commoner strips off the abandoned baby's clothes, he is self-righteously arguing that someone else would come along and take them away. But even he needs self-justification. He claims that the baby's parents "had a good time making it, then they throw it away like this," implying that the parents' evildoing is a license for his own. The commoner's bold cynicism brings clarity to the situation and breaks the spell of lies. The woodcutter sees now how ugly stealing is, especially from someone as helpless as a baby — or a dead samurai — and he repents. "I am the one who ought to be ashamed," he says after the commoner has gone.

Nothing of this sort was in Akutagawa's short story. Not only is the commoner's character new, but so is the whole moral dimension. "In a Grove" leaves one with the feeling that all truth is relative, unknowable, and perhaps even nonexistent. The idea of the relative nature of truth is carried over into the script, but here the revelation of truth is possible: it happens in the experience of the woodcutter. In the script, Akutagawa's pessimism is turned into belief that, despite man's weakness and vice, the human heart is capable of noble emotions and that, although evil is everywhere, good seems to find its way through.

The woodcutter takes in the abandoned baby. The balance between good and evil is restored. "Thanks to you," says the priest, "I think I will be able to keep my faith in men."

The introduction of the commoner is important also for the structure of the plot. The commoner asks the priest and the woodcutter many questions: "What's the matter?" "What can't you understand?" "Why don't you tell me about it?" "Why don't you tell the police?" "What was the bandit doing?" "What kind of story did she tell?" "Anything else you want to tell me?" Simple as they are, the commoner's questions become an active force in bringing together the different fragments of the events. The questions act as a catalyst; they facilitate the constant switching of locations, the movement from past to present and from present to past.

"In a Grove" provided the screenwriters with the mysterious crime and most of the characters. The contribution of the Akutagawa's second story, "The Rasho Gate," was no less important to the script, although it is not as obvious.

The story takes place in eleventh-century Kyoto, the medieval capital of Japan, devastated by wars, disease, and natural calamities. Under the half-ruined and gloomy Rashomon—the largest gate in the city—a samurai's servant took shelter from the wind and the rain. He had no place to go—his master could no longer afford to keep him. The servant was lost in thought: should he remain honest and die of hunger? Should he become a thief and survive?

The chill of the stormy night forced him to climb the stairs to the tower above the gate. By the light of a torch, he could distinguish many corpses, among them, a shriveled old woman kneeling next to the body of a woman with long hair. Strand by strand she was pulling out the hair. The servant was horror-struck and repulsed. Death seemed preferable to stealing, especially stealing from the dead—similar to the feelings of the woodcutter in the *Rashomon* script as he witnesses the commoner's "kneeling over the baby, stripping off its clothes."

Bringing the blade of the sword "before her very nose," the servant demanded an explanation from the old woman. Trembling and frightened, she told him she did it to survive. She would make a wig and then sell it. The dead woman had not been decent either—she used to sell dried snakes, saying they were dried fish. "If she hadn't been doing it, she would have starved to death." This same immoral logic also inspired the commoner's thinking in *Rashomon*.

Akutagawa describes how the servant, listening to the old woman, was ready to become a thief. He seized the old woman by the neck and told her he was going to rob her to survive. "He tore her clothes from her body and kicked her roughly down onto the corpses as she struggled and tried to clutch his leg." With her clothes under his arm, he "rushed down the steep stairs into the abyss of night." This action parallels that of the commoner in *Rashomon* when he leaves with the baby's clothes. "The baby starts to cry. The commoner glares at it; then, laughing, he turns to go . . . out into the rain."

Besides the psychological patterns of the story that were applied to the script, the images of the gate and of the rain were strongly influential. Akutagawa describes how "foxes and other wild animals made their dens in the ruins of the gate, and thieves and robbers found a home there, too. Eventually it became customary to bring unclaimed corpses to this gate and abandon them there. After dark it was so ghostly that no one dared approach." In the five-page story, Akutagawa mentions the rain more than ten times: its severity, its sound, its chill, its endlessness. The script intensifies this almost mythological scene of the heavens opening up and of devastation and abandonment, but it makes the image of the Rashomon more laconic—no animals, no corpses, just the gigantic eerie ruin under the unrelenting torrential rain.[8]

The action in the script unfolds in three locations: the gate, the courtyard, and the grove. Unlike the gate, the courtyard is not described by Akutagawa at all. He only mentions it indirectly. Likewise, in the script there are only a few remarks about the tribunal courtyard wall and about the sandy ground within. Those sparse strokes in the script, however, make the space real. In the film, the courtyard space looks empty but for an endless horizontal line, which is the edge of the wall. Not one detail draws attention away from the testimonies. The grove too is described by Akutagawa only a few times, either in short remarks, "a grove . . . of bamboo and cedars," or as a poetic image, "the light gradually grew fainter, till the cedars and bamboo were lost to view." In the script, though, the space is seen constantly—"a road winds through a bamboo grove," "a small brook," "a hill," "the bushes," "the sky and the trees," "the dazzling light of the sun breaks through the branches of trees," the bandit runs "through some woods," the woodcutter walks "through a dense woods," the police agent runs "along the bank" of the river, and the woman dips "her hand in the water" of "a small brook." (As noted, space in scripts is always concrete and specific.)

Each of the three locations in *Rashomon* has a very distinct image, mood, and texture. The huge, gloomy gate is enveloped in a downpour. The grove has a density of trees, light, shadow, and emotional tension. The courtyard has bare ground and a plain white wall.

Of the twenty-nine scenes that constitute the script, five are located at the gate, ten at the grove, and twelve at the courtyard. There are only two short scenes whose textures differ—the riverbank, where the police agent arrests the bandit, and the lake, in which the woman wants to drown herself.

How the script activates the static space of the two short stories by intercutting among three textures can be seen easily in a diagram. The ⇑ stands for the gate; ♣ for the grove; ⊟ for the courtyard, ⊵ for the riverbank; and ⬚Q⬚ for the lake.

```
⇑♣⊟♣⊟⊵⊟♣⊟♣⊟♣⊟♣⊟⇑⊟♣⊟♣⊟Q⊟⇑⊟♣⇑♣⇑
1 2 3 4 5 6 7 8 9 10 11 12 13 14 15 16 17 18 19 20 21 22 23 24 25 26 27 28 29
```

Notice the constant location changes: from the intense passions in the grove, to the sober emptiness of the courtyard, to the gloomy, entrapped atmosphere of the gate. This shifting heightens curiosity, not so much about who killed the samurai as about the conflicting impulses and inexplicable behavior of the characters, which is the main source of tension in *Rashomon*. Why does the woman plead guilty if she did not stab her husband? If she did stab him, why has she risked her life for him by attacking the bandit? The bandit, famous for his atrocities, readily admits the crime. Does this admission mean that he is honest? If he did not kill the samurai, why does he invite punishment for himself? Out of honor? And as for the dead samurai, what disturbs his eternal rest? If he did not commit suicide, what drives him to invent his story now? Unlike the other characters, the woodcutter wants to hide his actions because he is afraid of the police. Still, he too would like to consider himself nobler than he really is.

Piecing together different moments of the drama, making comparisons, observing, alternating from one version to another, believing them all, and then doubting them all, one arrives at the same conclusion that Kurosawa formulated in his memoirs: "Human beings are unable to be honest with themselves about themselves. They cannot talk about themselves without embellishing. This script portrays such human beings—the kind who cannot survive without lies to make them feel they are better people than they really are."

The *story* of a script, as well as of a novel, is a totality of events taken in chronological order.[9] The story in the *Rashomon* script unrolls as follows:

1. the samurai and his wife pass the priest on the road
2. the bandit sees them
3. the rape occurs
4. the samurai is killed
5. the police agent arrests the bandit
6. the witnesses and participants in the drama testify in the courtyard
7. the priest and the woodcutter seek shelter under the gate
8. they meet the commoner and discuss the events that happened in the courtyard that morning, some hours earlier
9. they hear the abandoned baby's cry
10. the commoner steals the baby's clothes and leaves
11. the woodcutter takes the foundling to his family

Thus, the story reveals, first, everything that happened in the grove; second, the action in the courtyard; and third, what happened under the

Rasho gate. The *story duration* is three days. It is measured from the earliest to the latest chronological points—from when the priest has met the couple until the woodcutter leaves the Rasho gate with the abandoned baby.

The *plot* arranges the story's events in the most expressive way. In *Rashomon,* the plot disrupts the chronological continuity of the story and develops a temporal order of its own. The *plot duration* is different from the story duration; it is much shorter.

Note in the following diagram of the twenty-nine scenes how completely restructured, dynamic, and active the chronological order of the plot is. The diagram shows the constant changes of location, describes the action, and places events in time.

1		The priest, the woodcutter, and the commoner are under the Rashomon. The woodcutter starts to recount what happened three days ago in the grove.	The present
2		The woodcutter finds the corpse in the woods.	Three days prior
3		The woodcutter and the priest are testifying in the courtyard.	Morning of the present day
4		The priest meets the samurai and his wife on the road in the woods.	Three days prior (earliest point)
5		The priest and then the police agent testify in the courtyard.	Morning of the present day

6		The police agent catches the bandit at the riverbank.	Two days prior
7		The police agent and the bandit are in the courtyard. The bandit testifies that he killed the samurai.	Morning of the present day
8		The bandit sees the couple in the woods.	Three days prior
9		The bandit says that his view of the woman "was just a glimpse of an angel."	Morning of the present day
10		The bandit lures the samurai into the grove, ties him to a tree, and runs to the road to tell the woman that her husband was bitten by a snake.	Three days prior
11		The bandit says in the courtyard that the sight of the woman made him "jealous of the man. I started to hate him."	Morning of the present day
12		The bandit and the woman run through the woods. When she sees what happened to her husband, she attacks the bandit with her dagger but finally succumbs.	Three days prior

13		The bandit testifies that he did not intend to kill the samurai.	Morning of the present day
14		The woman wants to belong to the winner. The bandit and the samurai fight, and the bandit kills the samurai. Meanwhile, the woman has disappeared.	Three days prior
15		In the courtyard, the bandit says that the woman turned out to be like any other, so he did not look for her. His biggest mistake was that he forgot about her dagger.	Morning of the present day
16		The priest, the woodcutter, and the commoner are discussing what happened in the grove. The priest says that they saw the woman in the courtyard.	The present
17		The woman testifies that, after taking advantage of her, the bandit left the grove.	Morning of the present day
18		In the grove, the samurai looks at his wife with hatred.	Three days prior
19		In the courtyard, the woman says that she cannot forget her husband's eyes, full of cold hatred.	Morning of the present day

20		The woman asks the samurai to kill her but not to look at her "like that." She has a dagger in her hand.	Three days prior
21		The woman testifies in the courtyard that she fainted, and when she opened her eyes, the dagger was in her husband's chest.	Morning of the present day
22		A lake is illuminated by the sun. The woman's offscreen voice claims that she tried to kill herself but failed.	Three days prior
23		In the courtyard, the woman asks, "What should a poor helpless woman like me do?"	Morning of the present day
24		The priest, the woodcutter, and the commoner continue discussing the events of the grove. The commoner says that the more he hears the more confused he is.	The present
25		The dead samurai testifies through a medium that the bandit, after attacking his wife, tried to console her.	Morning of the present day
26		The bandit is shocked when the woman asks him to kill her husband and is ready to punish her. The woman runs away. After the bandit leaves the grove, the samurai thrusts the dagger into his own chest.	Three days prior

27		The woodcutter protests and says that the samurai was killed by a sword. The commoner figures out that the woodcutter has witnessed the murder and insists that the woodcutter tell all about it.	The present
28		The woodcutter tells about the samurai's refusal to fight "for such a woman," but he and the bandit fight rather pathetically in the grove, and the bandit kills the samurai. The woman flees into the woods.	Three days prior
29		The commoner steals the abandoned baby's clothes and leaves the gate. The repentant woodcutter takes the baby. The priest claims that the woodcutter has restored his faith in mankind. With the baby cradled in his arms, the woodcutter leaves the Rashomon.	The present (latest point)

Looking at the first and final scenes in the diagram, it is clear that the plot duration is only the several hours spent under the gate. The grove and the court scenes are inserted into the present as flashbacks. Note that the plot condenses the three-day duration of the story into several hours; in turn, the *screening time* condenses the plot duration into eighty-eight minutes. (Although the screening time of *Rashomon* was finalized in the editing room, where every shot's length was determined exactly, the guidelines for the length of the entire film and of its parts were determined by Kurosawa and Hashimoto when they were developing the plot of the script.) Screening time, plot duration, and story duration—the three categories of time—are of supreme importance in screenwriting.

The diagram clearly reveals the temporal mosaic of the script's scenes. The story's chronological continuity is broken up into pieces and then put together in a completely different succession: the first scene starts in the present; the second is moved to the past—three days prior; the third scene takes place in the morning of the present day; the fourth, again, three days ago, and so on.

The jumps in time give *Rashomon* its dramatic intensity. Because the samurai's corpse is seen (scene 2) before the samurai and his wife are seen traveling through the woods (scene 4), the audience is more alert than they would have been if the events had appeared in chronological order. The audience is more focused on the characters' reactions than on the events themselves, which is what the screenwriters want. Otherwise they would not have repeated the same action several times.

There are many other instances in which the authors alienate the audience from the action and draw attention to human nature in general by presenting in succession episodes taken out of their original continuity. For example, the bandit's account of the rape and murder is interrupted several times by the courtyard scenes (9, 11, 13, 15), which removes the audience emotionally from the space and time of the drama again and again. The audience is forced to evaluate the drama rationally and to contemplate it from a distance.

If the gate scenes are singled out, as in the following diagram, the role of their position becomes clear. They frame the rape-murder drama; they constitute the beginning and the end of the script; and one of the gate scenes (scene 16) marks the middle of the script.

⚭															⚭											⚭		⚭	
1	2	3	4	5	6	7	8	9	10	11	12	13	14	15	16	17	18	19	20	21	22	23	24	25	26	27	28	29	

The first half of the script focuses on the interplay between the events in the grove and the investigation in the courtyard. In the second part of the script, the gate scenes appear more frequently. From being just supportive to the grove drama, the gate scenes become a drama in themselves. A parallel is subtly drawn: in both dramas there are three participants, among them one villain (in the grove, the bandit; at the gate, the commoner). There are also similarities between the gate and the courtyard scenes: in both a trial is under way, but the trial at the gate is more successful; it is here, not at the court, that the truth is revealed—the commoner figures out that the woodcutter stole the dagger, and the woodcutter is truly repentant, "I am the one who ought to be ashamed" he admits.

The plot of *Rashomon* destroyed the temporal order of the events as they were originally written. But another unity between the scenes was established. The textures of space and discontinuous time have been composed into a meaningful artistic whole. The drama at the gate has become a continuation of the drama in the grove.

The last scene, in which the woodcutter adopts the baby, brings a positive finale to the entire script. Now faith in human kindness and compassion is restored. The ego as a source of misdeeds is balanced by this act. At the very end of the script, the priest summarizes this change by saying to the woodcutter that, thanks to him, "I think I will be able to keep my faith in men." The priest and the woodcutter "bow to each other. . . . The woodcutter, holding the infant, leaves the gate; the sky is clear. . . . sunny." In Kurosawa's and Hashimoto's adaptation, "the sunny sky," symbolizing hope and goodness, was added to the gloomy and hopeless world of Akutagawa's short stories.

7.
Details, Motifs, and the Director's Commentaries

Viridiana
by Luis Buñuel and Julio Alejandro

Viridiana, 1961
    Director: Luis Buñuel
Screenplay: Luis Buñuel
               Julio Alejandro

Luis Buñuel (1900–1983) began his career in 1929 when he collaborated with another Spaniard in Paris, his friend Salvador Dalí, on the infamous film *Un Chien andalou*. "I decided to take the aesthetics of Surrealism to the screen,"[1] wrote Buñuel many years later. He found film to be "the best medium to show a reality which we cannot actually touch with our hands in everyday life."[2] *Un Chien andalou* established Buñel's style as one of the most daring and provocative in the history of cinema.

    Because of his fierce iconoclasm, the director's films often stirred controversy. They were frequently banned or censored, or they provoked boycotts. Buñel's reputation made it difficult for him to obtain funding for his projects, and along with economic and political factors, this may explain the period of fourteen years (1933–47) when he produced no films at all. Much of this time was spent in Hollywood, where Buñuel was dubbing films for Paramount and Warner Brothers, and in New York, where he worked in the film archives at the Museum of Modern Art.

After World War II, Buñuel returned to making movies mostly in Mexico then later in France. These films were in a decidedly more narrative vein than had been his earlier works, but they were no less dedicated to the expansion of cinematic expressiveness and boldness. Buñuel used to say that it was no longer possible to scandalize people in the second part of the century—one now had to do it with sweet subversion. With his films, among them *Los Olvidados, Nazarin,* and *Belle de Jour,* Buñuel proved that surrealism was not merely a fashionable craze of the 1920s and 1930s but a sophisticated aesthetic movement ideally suited to film.

In 1960, after twenty-four years in exile, Buñuel returned to his native Spain to make *Viridiana.* His return was seen as a betrayal by some political refugees. Yet one can imagine the temptation that this project held for him: his producer offered him a generous budget; mostly professional actors, although some members of *Viridiana*'s flock of beggars were indeed beggars, most notably the man who plays the leper; and complete artistic control—advantages that Buñuel had rarely enjoyed in his previous films. Working quickly, as usual, he shot *Viridiana* in a couple of months. Buñuel wrote the script with some help from his friend Julio Alejandro. The story is based loosely on the life of an obscure saint and on one of Buñuel's lingering erotic fantasies.

The customary uproar surrounded the release of *Viridiana.* It caused an immediate scandal with Franco's censors, as well as with the Catholic church. The film was eventually banned in Spain and in Italy, where Buñuel was threatened with an automatic prison sentence if he entered the country. The film was hotly debated by European and American critics, especially for its theological themes. *Viridiana* was understood to be either a film that showed the absence of God, as some critics thought, or one that questioned the manner in which God is worshipped, as some others argued. Despite the confusion, however, *Viridiana* took the Golden Palm at the Cannes Film Festival that year, the first major prize ever earned by the Spanish cinema. Today the film is considered one of the world's cinema classics.

Buñuel's popularity increased steadily over the years as his audience caught up with him and as his attitude mellowed somewhat. In fact, his relatively playful *The Discreet Charm of the Bourgeoisie* won the Oscar in 1973 as best foreign film, finally signaling his acceptance in America.

The camera has a natural eye for detail. There is no other tool that captures details so impressively. The camera is able to move in on an image (a house, for example), come closer and closer to a selected part (a window), and by enlarging it to the size of the screen, isolate it from the rest of the picture. This movement is such an essential cinematic technique that it can be said that the language of film was born when D. W. Griffith started moving the camera in and out and, in 1908, brought it directly toward the face of a heroine in the film *After Many Years*.[3] Since that time, singling out one detail of an image has become a powerful device in cinematic storytelling.

A close-up can turn any object (or part of it) into detail in film. Sometimes a close-up is done for purely visual purposes, and this detail would pertain mainly to the director's shooting style; but sometimes a close-up is originated in the script—it is a detail that contributes to the plot, the development of a character, the statement of a theme, or any combination of these.

In *Notorious,* the wine cellar key is crucial to the plot of the film; significant attention is paid to it in the screenplay and in the film. The close-up on the key is one of the most suspenseful moments in the film. The key is stealthily passed among Sebastian, Alicia, and Devlin. Through their relationship to the key, the audience learns something about each of them.

In *La Strada,* the close-up on the eyes of Osvaldo, an isolated, retarded child, and later, the close-up on the almost identical eyes of Gelsomina reveal without words Fellini's thoughts about the similarity of these two people who cannot comprehend the surrounding world.

Perhaps no other filmmaker has been as adept at telling his stories through details as has Luis Buñuel. *Viridiana* is the best example of this skill. His obsessive repetition of particular details not only enhances the plot but reveals some of his personal ideas about art, religion, life, death, and eroticism.

Synopsis

At the urging of her mother superior, Viridiana, a young Spanish novice, reluctantly agrees to visit her aging uncle, Don Jaime. She has never been close to him or seen much of him.

Don Jaime lives alone in an old mansion. His faithful servant Ramona, a young woman with a seven- or eight-year-old daughter named Rita, takes good care of him.

When Viridiana appears at Don Jaime's estate, she is cool toward her uncle. She tells him quite frankly that she would have preferred not to visit. Don Jaime is hurt by her honesty. He remarks that she closely resembles her aunt, his deceased wife, Doña Elvira. Now his interest in the young girl obviously goes beyond the familial.

The next day, Viridiana voices her disapproval of Don Jaime's indifference to his illegitimate son, Jorge, whom he has always taken care of but has never actually seen. Viridiana thinks this disinterest is evil.

Over the next few days, with Ramona's help, Don Jaime does some spying on his niece. Ramona reports that Viridiana has strange bedtime habits: the young woman sleeps on the floor, although a fine bed has been provided, and she worships at a makeshift shrine composed of the instruments of the crucifixion.

Don Jaime has his own fixations, and one evening, while trying to squeeze himself into his late wife's trousseau, he is distracted by Viridiana's sleepwalking. He follows her and watches as she dumps the contents of a sewing basket into the fireplace and then refills the basket with ashes, which she then deposits on her uncle's bed next to her aunt's wedding veil. Later, when Don Jaime recounts the details of her somnambulism, Viridiana interprets them as an omen of penance and death.

The final day of Viridiana's visit arrives. Don Jaime has grown mad for his niece and is desperate for her to stay. He seeks Ramona's help, and she is willing to oblige any of his wishes. He calls her attention to a vial of pills that he keeps in a cupboard.

Viridiana has warmed up to her uncle since her arrival, and she admits that he is a good man. Now that Don Jaime has won her over, he requests one small favor before she leaves.

Dressed in the wedding gown that Don Jaime modeled earlier, Viridiana bears an exact resemblance to the portrait of her aunt. She is amused at her uncle's seemingly harmless last wish. But when Ramona blurts out that her uncle would like to propose marriage, Viridiana is appalled. Ramona offers her some coffee to calm her nerves, and she soon passes out from the drink.

Don Jaime arranges Viridiana on her aunt's bed. She looks to be at once a virgin bride and a corpse. He wrestles with his conscience: now that he has Viridiana in such a vulnerable position, can he go through with his sinister plan? He kisses her once and then, overcome with revulsion at his own deed, hurries out of the room.

The next morning, while Viridiana is still in bed, in a twisted ploy to convince her to stay, Don Jaime tells her that he took full advantage of her helplessness the night before. She is horrified at the thought. Once again he tries to elicit Ramona's help in persuading his niece, but the servant has her own designs on Don Jaime and would prefer to see Viridiana go back to the convent. Don Jaime later tells Viridiana that he had lied, he had not taken advantage of her. Viridiana does not know what to believe, and she rushes out of the house.

Just as she is about to board the bus, Viridiana is stopped by the police and informed that she must return to the estate because of an emergency. When she arrives, she discovers that Don Jaime has hanged himself from a tree.

When the mother superior comes to pay her respects, Viridiana tells her that she feels responsible for her uncle's suicide and that she will not be returning to the convent. She will carry out her duties to God in her own private way.

Viridiana goes to the village and gathers together a group of beggars, prostitutes, and tramps. She plans to take them back to the estate to live. In the meantime, Jorge, Don Jaime's illegitimate son, has arrived along with his girlfriend, Lucia. He seems to have big plans for the land that his father has left to him and Viridiana. When Viridiana arrives with her band of unfortunates, she casts an unusual impression on her cousin and his companion.

Jorge's presence makes Ramona nervous, and she spills the soup that she was to serve for dinner. She has fallen in love with him at first sight. Lucia is suspicious of the source of the maid's jitters.

In the shed where the beggars eat, Viridiana introduces two new members to her group. One of the new recruits is a leper, and the other beggars instantly call for his removal. But Viridiana insists that he stay and that the others "treat him like a sick brother."

In the field, the leper traps a dove with his hands. "My darling, sweet dove," says he, putting the bird inside his jacket.

Jorge openly disapproves of Viridiana's personal brand of philanthropy. In turn, Viridiana shows no interest in Jorge's modernization efforts. However, the two are able to tolerate each other's preoccupations for a short time.

Lucia is jealous of Jorge's interest in Viridiana and tired of being ignored by him, so she leaves the estate. Jorge is indeed attracted to Viridiana. But soon he and Ramona become lovers.

Viridiana and Jorge must meet with their lawyer in town. They must also take Ramona and her daughter, Rita, with them so that the little girl can visit the dentist. Viridiana leaves her keys with the most responsible of the beggars. But almost as soon as they are gone, the beggars break into the mansion.

The beggars lay a sumptuous feast for themselves, using the finest foods, wines, silver, and linens that the house has to offer. Even the leper is included, although he sits at a small separate table. They have quite a festive time.

Suddenly, a vicious fight breaks out between two of the women, and some household valuables are upset. The leper dons the veil and corset of Don Jaime's deceased wife and plays "The Hallelujah Chorus" on the phonograph. A mad dance ensues. When a blind beggar hears that his woman, Enedina, is betraying him somewhere in the room with the beggar Poca, he goes on a rampage, smashing things with his cane. The party is cut short by the return of the owners.

When Jorge finds Hobbly, the crippled beggar, in his room, he orders him to go, but the intruder pulls a knife on him. From behind, the leper hits Jorge with a bottle, knocking him unconscious. When Viridiana stumbles onto this scene, she is shocked. Meanwhile, Ramona senses that something is wrong inside the house and orders the driver to take her back to town so that she can alert the police.

Hobbly locks Viridiana in a powerful hold. She appeals to the leper for help, but he sees some advantage in the situation and ignores her. Instead, he begins to tie up Jorge. Viridiana struggles furiously with her adversary, but she almost faints when she realizes that the rope he is wearing as a belt is the same one with which her uncle hanged himself. As Jorge regains consciousness, he offers the leper money to kill Hobbly. The leper is torn between the attraction of the money and the chance to have Viridiana's body for himself. He finally picks up a fireplace shovel and delivers three hard blows to the back of Hobbly's head. Ramona arrives at that instant with the police.

Some time later, Jorge has had electricity installed in the house, and a great change has also occurred in Viridiana. She is no longer dressed as a peasant but in more refined, feminine clothes. She looks at herself in the mirror, the first sign of vanity she has yet displayed. The crown of thorns to which she once prayed burns in a fire outside her room.

At the mansion, Viridiana knocks at Jorge's door and interrupts his cozy encounter with Ramona. Jorge realizes that the opportunity to break through Viridiana's chastity has at last arrived.

He leads her to a card table where he and Ramona are about to begin a game. Both women seem uncomfortable with the situation,
but Jorge succeeds in calming them. As he deals the deck, he triumphantly announces, "I always knew that someday I would play
cards with my cousin Viridiana."[4]

Early in the script, Buñuel establishes the pattern of introducing his
characters by focusing on their legs and feet.

Private park. Close-up of the dirty, skinny legs of little Rita who is
jumping rope. They come forward and go backward, opening and
shutting like compasses. Rita jumps from one bare foot to the other. Nearby, behind her, the legs of a man are seen passing. As they
recede, the chest, then the face, of Don Jaime appear. He watches
the little girl's legs.

In the next scene, when Viridiana arrives, Buñuel further develops
this feet-legs motif.[5]

The camera frames the legs of Viridiana and Don Jaime, who are
moving forward side by side. They stop occasionally, as people do
when they are walking and talking together. At first we only hear
their voices. Then the camera shows them both completely. The
tone of the conversation is normal, except that Don Jaime's voice
shows evident interest. Hers has less expression.
DON JAIME: How long are you staying?
VIRIDIANA: A very short while, Uncle. I've been given permis-
             sion to stay only a few days.
DON JAIME: Was that difficult to get?
VIRIDIANA: No. Mother Superior told me to come.
Don Jaime stops.

Buñuel is defying the conventions of framing. In doing so, he gives a
rather bland expository exchange of dialogue an amusing twist: instead of
watching the facial expressions of two people talking to each other, the
audience is given the "expressions" of their feet and legs in their
movement, position, and shape.
The "feet-legs" motif recurs constantly in *Viridiana:* "Don Jaime's
feet [are] slowly working the pedals of a harmonium." As Viridiana
undresses, "her legs, white and perfectly shaped, appear in full light."
Don Jaime tries to squeeze his foot into one of his deceased wife's slippers.
When Viridiana is sleepwalking, Don Jaime is "visibly agitated" by the

sight of her bare legs. After a hard day's work, Jorge soaks his feet in a tub of hot water. And, "A big tree, through whose foliage hang the feet of a man."

After all those walking or jumping feet there is a variation in the motif: the frightening image of death—the motionless feet of Don Jaime hanging in midair. Now the motif reaches its culmination.

Almost immediately after the suicide scene, Buñuel gives an ironic turn to the motif. Rita's legs skip rope under the tree. Buñuel makes it clear that this is the same tree and the same jump rope used in the suicide.

Although the subtlety of comparing feet and legs is impressive and intriguing, the repetition of the motif has hardly any bearing on the development of the story in *Viridiana*. In retelling the script (or the film), one may freely exclude any reference to it. Buñuel is doing more than developing the story, he is injecting his bold and ironic commentary. The notorious surrealist "discusses" what is going on both in the story and in his mind. By focusing on feet, he effectively stands perspective on its head and makes his avant-garde point: why be traditional and characterize a person by his or her face?

The nether extremities are also expressive. The way feet touch the ground reveals a great deal about a character. How energetic are young Rita's leaps—back and forth, back and forth. How uncertain and stilted Don Jaime's steps are, and how smugly the self-confident Jorge puts his feet in the bath. One sees the four fast-moving, unconcerned legs of a dog and the beating legs of a dying bee; the beautiful legs of Viridiana and the dead legs of Don Jaime; the legs of two beggars making love at the party, their legs "stick out behind one end of the couch. Sometimes hers on the top, sometimes his."

There is something else that for Buñuel makes feet and legs more important than faces. The face expresses a person's thoughts and feelings; the legs and feet reveal the unconscious, instinctual side of a person, that is, everything to which the surrealists give preeminence.

Objects are not symbolic in themselves. Buñuel infuses them with symbolic meaning by focusing on them and bringing them into the screenplay again and again. An example is a harmless, ordinary jump rope with wooden handles. The motif is first established when Don Jaime has given the jump rope to little Rita so he can watch her as she skips. Rita innocently tells Don Jaime that she likes this jump rope because "it's got handles."

The phallic image of the handles reappears later when Viridiana watches a manservant milk a cow in a barn. He offers to let Viridiana try it herself.

The suggestion amuses Viridiana, but she declines.

VIRIDIANA: But I wouldn't know how.

He insists.

SERVANT: I'll show you. Hold here.

He grasps a teat and motions Viridiana to take it. Hesitating, she finally does so timidly. She sits on the stool that the servant pushes toward her. She blushes. She begins pulling the teat. . . . Viridiana obviously finds the sensation of the teat in her hand unpleasant . . . [and] gives up the struggle with a gesture of disgust.

In another scene, Viridiana does hold the wooden handles when she skips rope with Rita.

The motif appears again when Don Jaime hangs himself with the rope—he is strangled by his own guilt about Viridiana. "The rope which is tied to the branch has a wooden handle. It is Rita's jump rope." The rope is seen again when Rita skips under the tree. Moncho, a servant, tries to stop her: she must not play under *this* tree.

Brutally he takes hold of the jump rope and tries to snatch it from her. Rita struggles with him fiercely.

RITA: Give it to me. It's mine! . . . Don Jaime loved to watch me skip.

The servant finally seizes the rope and throws it away. . . . He leaves. As soon as his back is turned, Rita picks up the rope and with the same liveliness begins to skip. The picture of her legs again.

Some time later, Hobbly finds the jump rope and "takes it to tie up his trousers." The rope makes its final appearance during the struggle between Viridiana and Hobbly.

Meanwhile, in the fight, Viridiana ends up by falling on the bed under Hobbly. Her arms flail furiously in resistance. Her clenched hand grips the cord that the beggar is using as a belt. It is Rita's jump rope, the same one Don Jaime hanged himself with. As her hand touches the handle of the rope, her gesture freezes. Then she lets go, dropping her arms as if giving up the struggle. Hobbly brutally turns her face to his and avidly kisses her.

For Viridiana, the rope is the ominous symbol of her inescapable, obscene fate, which has hounded her throughout her stay outside the convent. Notice also that the jump rope unifies the two highest dramatic points of the film: Don Jaime's suicide and the attack on Viridiana.

The jump rope is what surrealists call *an object with multiple uses*. The function of the rope is different for Rita, for Don Jaime, for Hobbly, and for Viridiana. The rope is continually transformed from a thing into a symbol. Its obviously phallic handles add an erotic overtone to death, guilt, violence, and untainted youth.

The repetition of a detail is also used by Buñuel to illuminate characters through their relationship to the same object. For instance, each situation in which Doña Elvira's trousseau is worn by a different person reveals something about that character.

> Interior of Don Jaime's room. Don Jaime is sitting in front of a large carved wooden chest which he has just opened. He seems to be concentrating but his expression is impassive. He is looking at the wedding attire he has kept, and judging from the cut of the clothes, they are the ones his dead wife, Doña Elvira, wore on her wedding day. Don Jaime gradually takes out the different parts of the outfit. He gazes at some of them for a moment; others he hardly looks at at all. There is the veil, the bodice, the skirt, the crown of artificial orange blossoms, the satin slippers.
>
> He looks at some of these voluptuously. He throws the crown of orange blossoms on his bed. He takes off his shoes and tries to put his bare foot into one of the delicate feminine slippers. Now he takes a satin corset with ribbons out of the chest. The chorus of the Ninth Symphony is still heard. With difficulty Don Jaime gets up and, with the corset in his hands, goes toward his mirror. He draws on the corset and gazes at his face. . . . As Don Jaime is standing in front of the mirror a sudden noise makes him start. He rapidly hides the corset which he had wrapped around him and goes to the door.

On Don Jaime, the trousseau becomes another of his fetishes, a sign of his perversity and his inability to escape his fantasies of the past.

When Viridiana models the gown for her uncle, she appears quite natural in it. "Viridiana who appears clothed in the wedding dress previously seen in Don Jaime's hands, leaves Doña Elvira's room. She is holding a lit candelabra in her hand. She advances as if walking to the altar. Although the situation is not to her liking, she is a little amused by it." The gown reflects Viridiana's beauty and purity; it is also the cause of her slight ambivalence about the situation and hints at the changed Viridiana who appears at the end of the film.

Finally, the gown is worn by the leper at the beggars' party.

> In the middle of the hubbub the leper appears at the door of Don Jaime's room in Doña Elvira's veil and corset. He begins to dance to the music of the Hallelujah Chorus. It is a wild grotesque dance,

with movements of the fandango and an expression of inane merriment. His incongruous toothless mouth makes it slightly sinister. He pulls tufts of feathers out from his jacket and throws them around the room onto the guests. His entry causes some surprise. . . .

LEPER   *throwing the feathers*: Little dove of the south. Little
            dove.

Now the trousseau is a grotesque sign of the leper, a man who defiles the symbol of the Holy Spirit by scattering a dove's feathers. Physically impure, vicious, ugly, infectious, he desecrates the purity of the snow-white ritual gown and makes a parody of the bride.

Looking at the dancing leper, one immediately recalls Don Jaime in the same trousseau and discovers that, although aristocratic, cultured, and sensitive, he has a similar streak of perversity.

The beggars' party continues. One of the women joins the leper. "The women scream and the men jeer. Soon the singer gets up and goes to dance with the leper. She takes off his veil and puts it around herself. It begins to look like a witches' sabbath." The woman puts on the ritual veil, which does not belong to her. But Viridiana did the same when Don Jaime asked her to.

Another unexpected parallel is that between Viridiana's giving herself to Jorge by joining him and Ramona in the card game and the "witches' sabbath" at the beggars' party. This analogy is even more convincing if one takes into consideration Buñuel's original ending of the script, which he eventually changed: in the first version, Viridiana joined Jorge and Ramona in bed. It seems that Buñuel wants to remind the audience that everything is relative, and who cares, anyway; that ugliness is no less intriguing and intense than beauty; that instinct is stronger than reason; and that life is irrational. Irrationality with precision,—as Buñuel's onetime friend and coauthor Salvador Dalí would say.

Just as Don Jaime has his fetishes, Viridiana has hers. She is obsessed with the symbols of the crucifixion and worships them in the quiet of the evening in the solitude of her room. When Jorge unexpectedly comes in to see her, Viridiana quickly hides the cross, the nails, and the crown of thorns in the same way that Don Jaime hurriedly removed and hid the corset the night he heard Viridiana sleepwalking. Buñuel draws a distinct parallel between the two characters. It is his way of commenting that Viridiana's religious beliefs are as much a vice as Don Jaime's sexual fantasies. Both characters (as the audience gathers from Buñuel's commentaries) are married to dead ideals. Don Jaime is destroyed by his;

Viridiana (Buñuel hints) narrowly escapes destruction. Instead, it is the fetishes that die in the end as Buñuel shows.

> Little Rita, her shoulders covered by the old blanket already seen on her, is sitting on a big stone near the fire. She is holding the crown of thorns dear to Viridiana, looking at it curiously. While she is handling it she pricks her finger and a drop of blood appears. She sucks it, and after looking sorrowfully at the crown of thorns she throws it onto the fire with an air of detachment. The crown of thorns very soon becomes a crown of fire. Jazz music.

Buñuel manages to overcome one of the script format's greatest hindrances—the expression of the screenwriter's "voice." Unlike the novelist, the screenwriter is unable to depart from the plot or from the dialogue or from the description of the action. The screenwriter does not even have the playwright's advantage of theatrical dialogue, with its poetic tendency or digressive monologues. On the other hand, as can be seen in the following script segment, the screenwriter does have a definite advantage because visual details can be manipulated. Jorge "is still very busy with his father's trinkets. He suddenly comes across a small jeweled crucifix. With his left hand, he gets hold of the little blade which is set into one side of it: the crucifix is in fact the handle of a dagger." Buñuel's voice here is straightforward, subversive, and boldly ironic.

In *Viridiana,* the combination of the religious and the sexual is frequent, with the sexual always taking over. It is the classical surrealists credo to put instinct above everything else.

In the script, there are several scenes with distinctly biblical connotations. Buñuel does not miss a chance to make comical or even sarcastic commentaries by drawing unlikely comparisons and unexpected parallels. For example, Hobbly, who later makes an attempt to rape her, asks Viridiana to pose for his painting of the Virgin Mary (a twisted parallel to St. Luke, who supposedly was the first to paint the Virgin). While Viridiana is sitting for the painting, she converses with a pregnant prostitute who does not know who the father of her expected child might be and does not care. Buñuel turns the virgin concept into a sly, dirty joke.

In a scene with Jorge, Ramona, and Lucia, there is another grotesque parallel—this time to Martha and Mary washing the feet of Christ.

> The sitting room at night. Close-up of a basin of hot water which is still steaming. In the water are the feet of Jorge, who has rolled up his trousers. He is dressed for the country. He is sitting on Don Jaime's special armchair and smoking one of his pipes. Lucia, sitting on a small low chair in front of him, has just finished polish-

ing his boots. They are silent. She looks at him now and then.

LUCIA *off*: Are you tired?

JORGE: I nearly walked my legs off today. *He rubs his legs.*
Pointing to the basin. That has done me good.

There is a silence. Ramona comes in with a towel in her hand. She hands it to Jorge and then looks at Lucia, who goes on wiping the boots which have been waxed.

RAMONA: Why don't you let me do that, miss?

LUCIA: Because I've got him into bad habits.

Jorge begins to dry his feet. The maid bends down to pick up the basin, gets up, and turns. She goes to the door but stops before going out.

An amusing sexual undercurrent runs through this scene. Ramona and Lucia (Martha and Mary) are competing for Jorge's (Christ's) attention. Meanwhile, he is distracted by thoughts of his cousin, Viridiana (the Virgin Mary).

Another example of a biblical theme, which Buñuel turns into a sexual joke, is his parody of the Last Supper and simultaneously of Leonardo da Vinci's glorified painting. The scene is the most elaborately executed piece in *Viridiana,* both in the script and in the film. It occurs during the beggars' banquet.

POCA: Enedina's going to take a picture. So we'll have a souvenir.

DON AMALIO: Where's the camera?

ENEDINA: It's a present from my parents.

They go to one side of the table. The leper places himself near the blind man, who sits in the middle. The blind man sits very straight, with his arms stretched out and his two hands on the table. The others arrange themselves on either side of him, striking different poses. In honor of the occasion Don Zequiel has come out of his stupor. When everyone is ready Enedina stands in front of them. She turns her back to the camera. In a flash the still scene suddenly conjures up the scene of another Supper. Enedina sweeps her very ample skirt up to her face. The photograph is taken. She chokes with laughter behind her skirt. They all relax their pose and break out into disordered babbling. The group comes to life again and the hubbub reigns supreme.

Note how strong the tone of this scene is. Not only do the beggars assume the positions of Christ and his apostles (with the blind beggar as Christ) but Enedina's obscene gesture intensifies the parody: once again the religious content is underscored with a dirty joke.

The beggars' party is the dramatic culmination of the film. Viridiana's ideas—about human brotherhood, charity, and moral improvement, every reason she did not go back to the convent, wanting to serve God in her own way—are all defiled and destroyed. The party, begun out of desire to taste the life of the rich and feast at their table, turns at first into drunken revelry and ultimately into a witches' sabbath, accompanied by Handel's "Hallelujah Chorus."

While Enedina and the beggar Poca are making love behind the couch, the blind beggar, Enedina's lover, starts smashing everything around him. "Overcome with rage the blind man clutches his cane and, facing the banquet table, lays about him with all his strength. His flaying creates havoc with the contents of the table. Wine, sauces, and puddings are spilled. Very soon the beautiful embroidered tablecloth becomes a battlefield of destruction. Poca and Enedina, terrified, get up from behind the couch." So crucial to the development of the plot, this scene, on a more sophisticated level, reveals the most important of Buñuel's commentaries: the only satisfaction people can find is in giving way to their instincts, freeing themselves from the straitjacket of moral and social norms. Nothing can be more exciting than crossing the borders of the forbidden.

In this scene, the voices of Buñuel the storyteller and Buñuel the commentator become one. What the beggars do to the mansion, Buñuel does to the traditions of religion and morality. Neither the beggars nor he know any boundaries.

8.
Screen Dialogue

Bicycle Thieves
by Vittorio De Sica and Cesare Zavattini

Bicycle Thieves, 1948
  Director: Vittorio De Sica
Screenplay: Vittorio De Sica
            Cesare Zavattini

Vittorio De Sica (1901–74) began his career as a film director in 1940 after he had already made a name for himself as an outstanding stage and screen actor. He was adored by the Italian public and called "the Italian Cary Grant" by the critics. He had also been successful as a stage director and as a popular performer of the songs from his films. He acted in more than 150 films, Italian and foreign, among them such famous works as Roberto Rossellini's *General Della Rovere,* Charles Vidor's *Farewell to Arms,* and Max Ophüls' *Madame de.* . . . He continued acting in films until the final years of his life. De Sica occasionally acted in his own films, and he often participated in the writing of their scripts.

The most important of De Sica's early films was *The Children Are Watching Us* (1942), which was the beginning of his work with screenwriter Cesare Zavattini. In the mid-1940s, after the liberation of Rome and the end of World War II, De Sica and Zavattini made *Shoeshine* (1946), a tragic story about two street boys. The film was received negatively in Italy, but abroad, especially in America, it was a resounding success. In Hollywood, it was awarded a special Oscar. Released two years later, *Bicycle Thieves*[1] (1948), with its socially conscious theme, its real-life setting, and its nonprofessional actors, became a classic of neorealism, the artistic and political movement of the 1940s, and brought the authors international fame. Almost as successful as *Bicycle Thieves* were De Sica's and Zavattini's *Miracle in Milan* (1951) and *Umberto D.* (1952).

Although De Sica continued making films through the 1970s *(The Gold of Naples; Yesterday, Today, and Tomorrow; Marriage Italian Style; The Garden of the Finzi-Continis; The Voyage),* none reached the height of his best early pictures. One of De Sica's last projects was a script for a film about Italian immigrants to America, which he planned to shoot in Brooklyn. It was to be his answer to *The Godfather.* The project was never realized: he died in 1974 in Paris on the day of the opening of *The Voyage.*

The novelist, publicist, and screenwriter Cesare Zavattini (b. 1902) was De Sica's lifelong collaborator. De Sica wrote, "When I am working on the creations of this tireless inventor of film stories, I follow the development of the plot step by step; I weigh, experience, discuss and define with him, often for months at a time, each twist and turn of the scenario. In this way, by the time we start shooting, I already have the complete film in my mind, with every character and in every detail. After such a long, methodical and meticulous inner preparation, the actual work for production boils down to very little."[2] Zavattini was the central figure of the neorealist movement. He insisted that film, art, and literature have social content, historical actuality, realistic treatment, popular setting, and political commitment on the part of the artist. Zavattini was a convinced and dedicated Marxist. In his articles and speeches, he maintained that the ideal film would be one in which real life is transferred directly onto the screen and that the main mission of a filmmaker is to observe and record reality and not to invent it. Yet everything in his best scripts is artistically organized and invented to the smallest detail. Among Zavattini's best scripts are those written for De Sica, as well as for Giuseppe De Santis *(Rome 11 O'clock,* 1952) and for Luchino Visconti *(Bellissima,* 1951).

In the 1960s Zavattini worked in collaboration with fifteen young directors on a documentary film about Rome. He was also active in supervising several films made in Cuba. But Zavattini the creative master found his demise along with the demise of neorealism in the latter half of the 1950s. By that time, neorealism had turned into a rigid dogma that stood in the way of further development of Italian cinema.

Bicycle Thieves was of special importance to both De Sica and Zavattini. Soon after the film was finished, Zavattini predicted that the rich would "turn up their noses" at it. But the opposite happened. The intellectual elite and the rich patrons of the arts were ecstatic about the film; it was the mass audience who did not want to accept it. De Sica once recalled that, during one of the first showings of the film in Rome, a working-class man asked the director for his money back—he wanted to be entertained not shown the misery of life.

De Sica always remembered with tenderness the making of the film and the people who worked with him on it: Ricci, who in real life was a metalworker from Breda; and especially Bruno, an eight-year-old son of refugees whom the director met by accident.

Dialogue exists within the visual nature of film and is subordinated to it. Therein lies the basic difference between theatrical plays, in which the emphasis is on words, and film, in which images are everything. A good film is always told in visual terms. The visual atmosphere of a film shapes the audience's perception of the words; and often the camera, with its position or movement, makes statements more profound than any spoken line.

There is a unique quality to film dialogue—the less said, the better— yet dialogue is an intrinsic element of film and of special concern to the screenwriter. The screenwriter listens carefully to how people of various professions, social classes, and ethnic groups speak and examines their vocabulary, expressions, speech mannerisms, and accents. But very little of what has been overheard can enter the script without change to become dialogue.

Dialogue and normal conversation are very different. A sentence from a conversation can rarely be transposed directly into film. Screen time is condensed, and the same must happen to dialogue. It must be cleared of anything random or secondary, of redundancies, ramblings, or empty words. In addition, characters in films do not simply talk to each other; their dialogue must contribute to the plot, which the author develops in a certain direction.

It is not easy to comprehend that film dialogue, like editing, lighting, and acting, is only an illusion of reality. Dialogue imitates everyday speech in its style, tone, and tempo but must fit the needs of the script, either by revealing a character or by emphasizing some nuance of the action.

Although every conversation in the script is carefully selected and directed toward a main dramatic goal, to the viewer it should sound perfectly real and colloquial. Good dialogue must give the impression of growing out of the action, or the illusion of reality may be destroyed.

Conciseness is one of the essentials of screen dialogue. Long speeches and monologues go against the dynamic nature of the cinema—they slow the action down. This necessary conciseness, in turn, gives rise to that particularly expressive, "coined" brand of phraseology used in film. It is no accident that certain lines of film dialogue have penetrated everyday speech almost as aphorisms, for example: "Go ahead—make my day"; "Play it again, Sam"; "Let's take him for a ride"; and "Frankly, Scarlett, I don't give a damn."

Good dialogue is not a result of the spoken lines alone; consideration must be given to its relation to the visual images and how harmoniously they work together. An important rule is that the word and the visual image must complement but not repeat each other. There is another rule as well: weak points in the structure of a screenplay should never be covered with lines of dialogue. The action should be further developed instead.

Analyzing the dialogue in the script of a master, one comes to realize that often it is not the actual words but the underlying meaning that is all important. In a scene from *Miracle in Milan*,[3] Lolotta, a fairy godmother, is dying. As her parting words to her beloved little son, Toto, she asks him the multiplication tables, as she used to do when she taught him arithmetic. Toto, in tears, holding her hands, answers her only in numbers, but in their dialogue the audience hears much more: Lolotta's adoration for Toto and his grief, fear, and love for her. The dryness of the numbers serves only to intensify, through contrast, the emotions. What matters is not what the characters say but what they mean.

In the case of the *Bicycle Thieves*—a script with a clear and simple plot—it is easy to see how film dialogue develops, how it reveals character, presents information, and moves the plot forward. In the script, the reader sees that dialogue can be either direct or oblique and elliptical and that the camera can unceremoniously inject itself into any conversation between film characters at any moment.

Synopsis

The year is 1946. A group of unemployed workers is waiting outside an office in a "drab, austere"[4] government housing project on the outskirts of Rome. They all hope to get a job. But only Ricci is lucky. Ricci's job, which begins the next day, is bill posting.

At a fountain, in a line for water, Ricci finds his wife, Maria. He tells her that he got a job, but to do it, he needs his bicycle. His bicycle, though, is at the pawnshop, and there is no money to redeem it.

Maria decides to pawn the last few things they have—the sheets they sleep on and the linens left from her trousseau.

At the pawnshop, Ricci and Maria redeem the bicycle, Ricci collects his uniform at the poster office, and they happily ride home.

As they turn on Via della Paglia, Maria asks Ricci to stop. She goes to see a woman. Ricci is waiting outside the building. After a while, he asks a group of boys to keep an eye on his bicycle and enters the building too.

The apartment of Signora Santona, the fortune-teller, is full of people. Awestruck, they are listening to her brief, cliché prophesies. Ricci tears his wife away from there. After she leaves some money for the fortune-teller, they go. Maria explains that Signora Santona had recently foretold that Ricci would get a job. Ricci is irritated that his wife can "be taken in by this foolishness."

Early the next morning, Bruno, Ricci's ten-year-old son, lovingly polishes the bicycle. He scolds his father for not noticing the dent that was not on the bike before they gave it to the pawnbroker. Maria, smiling, tells Ricci that in his new cap he looks handsome, like a policeman.

Ricci and Bruno are leaving together. Bruno, who is dressed in a worker's uniform similar to his father's, proudly imitates Ricci as they are getting ready. Before they leave, Bruno closes the shutters, so the light will not disturb his sleeping baby brother.

With Bruno on the handlebars, Ricci rides through the streets of Rome. At the gas station where Bruno works, he lets the boy off and tells him that he will pick him up at seven.

A workman teaches Ricci how to paste a poster on a wall. Ricci follows him, carrying a pail of glue. "If you leave any wrinkles and the inspector sees them, you're out," the man says.

On a busy street, Ricci stands on a ladder and tries to smooth out a Rita Hayworth poster. His bicycle is at the foot of the ladder. Three suspicious-looking men hesitate for a moment near the bicycle then continue on their way. Suddenly, one of them, a young man wearing a German army cap, comes back, jumps on Ricci's bike, and rides off. "Thief! Thief!" shouts Ricci, taking off after him. The thief's accomplice gets in Ricci's way, trying to block him. No one pays any attention to what is going on. Ricci hops into a passing car, explains to the driver what has happened, and the driver follows the bicycle. The chase through the traffic begins. But when they finally confront the rider, he turns out to be the wrong one.

At the police station, Ricci, very upset, tells an officer about the theft. The policeman is not impressed. "If you've got time you could try looking yourself," he tells Ricci.

Late in the evening, Bruno is waiting for his father at the gas station. Ricci gets out of the bus. He cannot bring himself to tell Bruno what has happened.

Biaocco, Ricci's friend, promises to help him search for the bicycle tomorrow at the marketplace at the Piazza Vittorio where "thieves sell the bikes as quickly as they can."

Ricci and Bruno drive to the Piazza Vittorio the next day in Biaocco's car. Bruno can describe the bicycle better than his father can. At the market, they split up—one will search among the tires, one among the frames. Bruno has to look at the bells and pumps. There are rows and rows of bicycles, as well as various parts. Their search is fruitless. They decide to go to another marketplace.

Ricci and Bruno get out of the car and hurry towards the stalls of the Porta Portese market. Suddenly, Ricci recognizes the thief in the crowd. He is handing some money to an old man. Shouting, "Thief!" Ricci dashes toward him. The thief blends into the crowd, so the father and son pursue the old man and confront him. The old man pretends that he does not know the thief and escapes into a church. Ricci and Bruno follow him; Ricci manages to get the thief's address from the old man. He wants the old man to go with them, but the old man slips away. Bruno criticizes his father for letting the old man get away. Frustrated and angry, Ricci slaps his son. He orders Bruno to wait on a bridge while he goes to look for the old man. Slowly and reluctantly, with tears in his eyes, Bruno moves toward the bridge.

Ricci walks along the riverbank. Suddenly, he hears cries for help—somebody has fallen into the river. Ricci runs toward the bridge, frightened that it is Bruno who fell.

Bruno is sitting quietly at the top of a staircase leading up to the bridge. Ricci catches sight of him. Short of breath, he runs up to his son.

Ricci takes Bruno to a café, and with what is left of the money, he orders some food. He discusses the family finances with Bruno, as with an equal. "Everything sorts itself out, except death," he concludes.

Ricci and Bruno go up the stairs to the fortune-teller's apartment. But Signora Santona's prediction does not help much. "Either you will find it immediately, or you will never find it," she says about the bicycle.

Back on the street, they practically bump into the thief, who recognizes them, dashes into the next street, then disappears into the doorway of a bordello. Ricci, with Bruno behind him, follows the thief into the place and drags him outside. A crowd of poor, angry people gathers. This neighborhood is the thief's. Here, everybody is against Ricci. They threaten to deprive him of "more than a bicycle."

The thief's mother accuses Ricci of persecuting her innocent son. In a sudden epileptic seizure, the thief falls to the ground. Meanwhile, Bruno disappears without anyone noticing.

The crowd tightens in an angry circle around Ricci. Someone is about to hit him, but at that moment Bruno comes back with a policeman.

The thief's mother asks the policeman to search her apartment. The bicycle is obviously not there. The policeman tells Ricci that he has no proof.

Father and son are walking down a street again near the stadium where a soccer game is going on. Outside the stadium, rows of bicycles are parked.

Seized with an idea, Ricci sends Bruno home and gives him some coins for the tram. Bruno crosses the street but misses the tram.

Ricci is standing near one of the bicycles that leans against a wall. In a flash, he grabs the bicycle and races off.

But he is not successful. The owner of the bicycle emerges from the doorway, shouting, "Thief! Stop him!" Several men chase Ricci. One of them manages to grab Ricci's coat. Ricci loses his balance and falls. More and more people gather around him. He is "defending himself against the blows and the insults."

Bruno, who witnessed everything, is horrified and runs to his father. Crying, he clings to Ricci's leg.

The owner of the bicycle looks at Bruno then at Ricci. He decides to let them go.

Slowly, Ricci and Bruno walk away.

Dialogue in *Bicycle Thieves* is used sparingly. Many of the spoken lines in the script are questions and answers, the simplest and most basic form of dialogue. While this form is sometimes overused by novices, in the hands of masters, it can be appropriate and necessary. In *Bicycle Thieves,* it is often not a spoken line, but an action, a gesture, or a camera movement that constitutes the question or the answer.

A screenwriter writing dialogue in some ways resembles a chess player who, while moving a piece, is thinking several moves ahead. Thus, at the beginning of the script, Ricci curses his fate when he thinks he may not be able to get his bicycle back from the pawnbroker. "I can always throw myself into the river." Later, after his argument with Bruno, he fears that his son has drowned. The audience recognizes this feeling — the idea of someone drowning in the river has already been implanted into a line of dialogue many "moves" ahead of time.

When Ricci sees the thief getting away on his bicycle, he shouts, "Stop him! Stop the thief. . . . Thief! Thief!" At the end of the script, the owner of the bicycle that Ricci steals shouts nearly the same words: "Thief . . . Thief . . . Stop him. Thief. Stop him!" This well-planned similarity expresses one of the main ideas of the film, how the honest, decent man can become a thief.

The dialogue in the script flows from the action, but at the same time, it is an active force in giving shape to the whole story, in structuring it as an artistic whole. Notice how the script begins: a clerk with a little cigar in his mouth, holding a handful of papers, is standing in front of a group of unemployed men.

> OFFICIAL *shouting*:   Ricci . . . Ricci . . . Where's Ricci?
> A MAN in the crowd reacts. He moves through the crowd looking for RICCI. Camera tracks with him as he leaves the group, running and shouting.
> WORKER: Ricci . . . Ricci . . .
> He runs towards the camera through the vast treeless expanse. An occasional poorly dressed resident passes in the foreground.
> WORKER: Ricci . . . Ricci . . .
> RICCI, sitting by a public fountain, looks up to see the MAN arrive.

When moved from script to film, the name, rhythmically repeated a number of times, sounds almost like a bell, which attracts the attention of the crowd in the film and the audience watching the film. It gives an active start to *Bicycle Thieves*. By organizing the beginning of the film in a way that contributes to the film's structure, the repetition of the protagonist's name serves a number of functions. While it resounds, the camera looks over the crowd, and the audience realizes that Ricci is one of them.

This motif, being part of a crowd, like everyone else, is brought out several times in the film. For example, when Ricci and Maria go to the pawnshop, the clerk puts their linens on a shelf among a number of other identical packages.

Throughout the film, Ricci is reminded that the world does not make exceptions for the plight of the individual. This dictum is first mentioned at the beginning of the film, when the official warns Ricci that, if he does not have a bicycle, he must give the job over to someone who does. It comes up again in the police station, when the policeman tells Ricci that they cannot set up a search for "just a bicycle." But the theme is dramatized most clearly at the fortune-teller's, when Bruno and his father jump the line of waiting patrons.

> BRUNO: Over here, papa . . . here's a seat free.
> BRUNO takes up his position in front of the chair just vacated by the MAN.
> CLIENT: Listen, boy . . . get back. . . .
> OLD LADY: Now, little one . . . wait your turn.
> ANOTHER LADY: Everyone must wait their turn. You must respect that. . . .
> RICCI *upset*:   I'm in rather a hurry, though.
> MAN: So am I in a hurry. . . .
> RICCI: But I really am in a great hurry.
> WOMAN: But we all are.
> RICCI: Please be kind enough to let me go first.
> ANOTHER WOMAN: It's extraordinary. There are always people who want to be first.

As the prostitute tells Ricci when he barges into the brothel after the young thief, "The law is the same for everyone." This line summarizes what Ricci has yet to understand; he does come to understand it when he, like the thief whom he tried to catch, steals a bicycle, and the crowd humiliates him. This callous, indifferent world does not make exceptions for his desperation and his problems.

Speech is usually an expression of a character's breeding, education, intelligence, and ethnicity. For instance, Ricci's and the thief's neighbors speak very differently from each other. The translation from Italian into English levels out this distinction. The neighbors use a southern Italian dialect—they are impoverished, recent immigrants to Rome; Ricci, in contrast, has a pure Roman pronunciation, underscoring the differences between them. At the same time, it adds dramatic impact to the moment when Ricci commits the same act as the man from that neighborhood.

De Sica and Zavattini deliberately juxtapose different types of speech to achieve greater expressiveness through contrast, as in this scene in the church, when Ricci and Bruno have run down the old man.

> REVEREND: Page six.
> He puts on his glasses and begins to read a prayer. Each of his phrases is repeated in litany by the faithful poor.
> REVEREND: I want to leave this holy place with a pure soul and a peace of mind. I try again to overcome the weakness of my flesh. . . .

The prayer continues off, and becomes indistinguishable in the background as the camera tracks along the rows of people and comes to a halt on RICCI and the OLD MAN.
RICCI: It's for his own good, this business. Where is he?
OLD MAN: I'm no informer. Leave me in peace.
RICCI: You know him. . . . If you don't tell me, I'll call the police.

The reverend's speech, so incongruous with Ricci's reality, only heightens his misery and dejection. The same is true for the confusing notions of Signora Santona, the fortune-teller.

SIGNORA SANTONA: What do you want, my son?
RICCI: Someone stole . . .
SIGNORA SANTONA: What did they steal?
RICCI: My bicycle!
SIGNORA SANTONA: Your bicycle. . . . What do you want me to tell you, my son? . . . I can't see what I can tell you. . . . I can only tell you what I see. . . . Listen . . . either you will find it immediately or you will never find it . . . Understand?
RICCI: Immediately? But where do I look?
SIGNORA SANTONA: I can tell you no more. Go and try to understand. Either you will find it immediately or you will never find it.

Her prophesy does little to clarify the situation; it only contributes to the atmosphere of inescapable failure and points to the futility of Ricci's efforts to solve the riddles of his fate. The very fact that Ricci consults Signora Santona, after telling his wife that only a fool would do so, is important for the plot. It is the start of Ricci's fall and the abandonment of his principles, which will culminate in his theft of a bicycle.

One of the most important functions of dialogue is to reveal character. For example, what Bruno says, how he says it, and what he does not say are expressions of his personality.

Medium long shot of the children's room in RICCI's apartment, early . . . morning. Close-up of a suspended bicycle wheel turning. Through the spokes, BRUNO, RICCI's son, who is about ten, is seen polishing the bike with great care. RICCI, in his uniform, enters the room.
RICCI: Hurry up, Bruno. . . . It's six-thirty.
BRUNO: I can't clean it very well in here. It's too dark still.

BRUNO . . . walks to the window and opens the shutters onto the feeble morning light. . . . RICCI moves towards his son. . . . BRUNO, polishing a pedal and looking unhappy.

Bruno is presented through what he is doing. His attachment to the bicycle is expressed physically ("through the spokes"). The following dialogue on the surface is about the bicycle, but its real function is to reveal Bruno's character.

BRUNO: Papa . . . did you see what they did?
RICCI *off*:   No . . . What?
BRUNO *furiously points to the pedal*:   A dent! . . .
RICCI: Perhaps it was there before . . .
BRUNO *enraged*:   No . . . it wasn't . . . I'm sure. You don't know how they look after things in there? You should have been more careful. . . . It's not them who pays for repairs, you know.
RICCI *laughing*:   Shhh . . . keep quiet.
BRUNO *cleaning and sulking*:   I'll keep quiet, but I'd have complained to them.

Everything Bruno says expresses the personality of a sensitive, responsible child who has matured before his time in the difficult postwar years in Rome. The dialogue also establishes their particular father-son, elder-younger relationship. Throughout the script, the reader sees the pattern of change in these roles; from time to time Bruno takes on the part of the "elder."

Thus, at the center of the story about Ricci and his bicycle is the story of Ricci and his son. It is the relationship between these two characters that is the most powerful part of the script. Just as certain clues, discoveries, and slipups take Ricci either closer to or farther away from his bicycle, so too do they take him closer to or farther away from Bruno. The tension in their relationship is sometimes expressed in dialogue. After they have lost track of the old man, there is an example of father-son confrontation.

BRUNO: I wouldn't have let him go for the food. . . .
RICCI: Oh . . . shut up, will you!

Ricci raises his hand and slaps Bruno. Crying, the boy runs away. The father takes a few steps after him.

BRUNO *sobbing*:   Leave me alone!
RICCI: Where are you going?

BRUNO: Back to the house. . . .

RICCI: Bruno, come over here. . . .

BRUNO: No . . . you hit me. . . .

RICCI: Come here at once.

BRUNO: No!

RICCI: Come here or I'll come and get you.

BRUNO: No. . . . I'm going.

RICCI *shouting*:   Bruno! . . .

BRUNO half-hidden behind a tree; RICCI standing about twenty feet away looking at him.

RICCI: Bruno . . . you're going to do as I say . . . do you understand . . . you impudent brat . . . come here. . . .

BRUNO: No. . . . I won't. . . . Why did you hit me?

RICCI: Because you were getting on my nerves. Now come along with me.

BRUNO: No . . . go by yourself.

RICCI . . . *furious*:   Bruno, you're going to obey me!

Although Bruno is probably right, he is still a child, subject to the control and temper of his father. Ricci is instantly sorry for what he has done but is unable to say so. Powerful emotions are left to silence.

In the scene after this exchange, Ricci mistakenly believes that Bruno has been nearly drowned, but then he sees his son waiting for him just as he had ordered him to do. The father-son reconciliation is conveyed through Ricci's words and Bruno's proud and silent sulking.

RICCI: Put your jacket back on, Bruno . . . you'll catch cold. . . .

They walk side by side across the bridge. RICCI tries to help BRUNO put the jacket on, but BRUNO insists on doing it without any paternal help. In the background, a small group of people look over the side of the bridge at the rescue operation. . . .

BRUNO is dragging his feet. RICCI eventually stops walking.

RICCI: You tired?

BRUNO looks down and nods his head, feebly. Then he looks over to a large stone block.

RICCI: Sit down there. . . . There's nothing else to do. . . . . We should go home. . . .

BRUNO sits on the stone as his father leans against the nearby wall. The shouts of a passing group cause them to look around.

VOICES: Viva Modena! Viva Modena! . . .

a crowd of young people are singing and shouting enthusiastically. . . .

> RICCI: Is Modena a good team? . . .
> BRUNO, a little less unhappy, but still unreceptive, shaking his head
> distastefully. . . .
> RICCI: Are you hungry? . . .
> RICCI: Could you manage a pizza?
> BRUNO's face lights up in assent.

The scene in the restaurant during a break in the search for the stolen
bicycle is of great significance. Ricci tells his son, "Everything sorts itself
out except death." He has just recovered from his fear for Bruno's life and
is filled with an understanding of how deeply he treasures his son. He
says, "Everything was going to be all right. . . . I'd worked it out. . . .
With the extras that we would make . . . let's see . . . yes . . . twelve
thousand . . . basic." By discussing finances with Bruno (an act of trust
and friendship), Ricci makes his ten-year-old son his equal. Nibbling on a
piece of cheese, Bruno writes on his paper napkin the numbers his father
dictates. "12,000 basic, 2,000 overtime, plus family allowances 800 by
30 . . . what does that come to?" While the mathematical computations
make for rather dry language, these numbers stand for Ricci's life, for his
dreams, and for his family's well-being. Once again, the importance lies
not in the words themselves but in the intentions implied behind the
words.

The final scene evokes this feeling once again. Even though the quest
for the bicycle has been fruitless, even though their efforts to improve
their life have resulted in nothing but disappointment, Ricci and his son
still have one another. There are no lines that could express the amount of
forgiveness and compassion in the image of Bruno reaching for his
father's hand. The search for the bicycle has, in the end, brought Bruno
and his father closer together. The writer and director of the film chose to
show this to the audience rather than tell it.

> Two men push RICCI forward. BRUNO stands alone near the tram
> rails. Now RICCI is caught and in custody, most of the crowd have
> resumed their strolling. BRUNO picks up RICCI's hat, dusts it off,
> and walks towards camera with tears running down his
> cheeks. . . . RICCI and his two guards across the parking lot. Be-
> hind them a handful of other men as well as the OWNER.
> MAN: Where do we take him?
> OWNER: There's a police station over there.
> MAN *off*:   Not all of us should go. Just a couple of witnesses and
> the owner . . . that's all.

> They stop walking as BRUNO runs up and grabs his father's
> legs. . . . RICCI looking down at his son. BRUNO looking up at his
> father. The OWNER watches both father and son. He seems fed up
> and deflated.
> OWNER: Come on. . . . I don't want to make trouble . . . not for
> anyone. . . . Let's just forget it.
> MAN *off*:   You ought to put him behind bars.
> OWNER: Let him go. . . . Good-bye and thank you all.
> He moves out of shot. BRUNO is drying his eyes.
> MAN *off*:   That's a nice trick to teach your son.

This last line of dialogue reveals much more than it says. Fitting for the
situation, it also summarizes the underlying meaning of the film—a child
receives a bitter lesson about the life of adults, and the paradise of his poor
but decent childhood, a childhood in which his father is idealized, is lost
forever.

In the last scene of the script, all the spoken lines belong to the owner
of the bicycle and some people in the crowd, but the focus is on Ricci and
Bruno. And the finale of the film is developed completely without
dialogue.

> RICCI and BRUNO walk slowly across the parking area. The sound
> of indistinct insults follows them. People walk by, as they do on
> any Sunday afternoon. BRUNO discreetly hands his father the hat.
> RICCI takes it and straightens his hair . . . his jaw set, eyes empty
> of emotion, shoulders sagging. . . . BRUNO hugging his father's
> legs, and still wiping the odd tear from his face. They move
> through the lolling crowd. . . . RICCI tries to hold back the tears in
> his eyes. He continues to walk with a faltering step. . . . BRUNO
> walking next to his father still looking up at him. . . . BRUNO's
> hand slipping into his father's. RICCI squeezes the hand. . . . RICCI
> walking on and crying; BRUNO holding his father's hand . . . they
> move away and disappear into the gathering crowd.

Before De Sica and Zavattini collaborated on *Bicycle Thieves,* they
made a film called *The Children Are Watching Us,* which would have been
an appropriate subtitle for *Bicycle Thieves.* Bruno watches his father and
at times imitates him throughout the film. Except for an occasional
remark, Bruno is mostly silent during the search for the bicycle, yet the
audience is always aware of his presence and of his role as more than an
innocent spectator in a harsh world. He represents an ethical point of view

in the film. At the end of the film, the audience sees Ricci's theft of the bicycle through Bruno's eyes, and this viewpoint is what makes the last scene so dramatic.

Silence is a form of dialogue, just as the pause is an essential part of musical composition. When it is appropriate, silence is one of the most effective methods a screenwriter can use to convey the emotions of the characters, and it is often the one used the least. The screenwriter must know not only how and what to write but also when to write nothing at all. With every line of dialogue the screenwriter should ask, Is there a way of showing this information instead of saying it? If there is, then by all means it should be shown. Film is a visual art, as such, the dialogue must always be secondary to the image. After all, a picture is worth a thousand words, perhaps more.

9.
The Screenplay as a Model for Literature

Kiss of the Spider Woman,
a novel by Manuel Puig

Kiss of the Spider Woman, 1976
A Novel by Manuel Puig

Manuel Puig's (b. 1932) obsessive interest in movies, especially Hollywood movies, developed at an early age in his native Argentina. He claims to have occupied the same seat in the local movie theater every day for ten years. Much later Puig wrote about Hollywood films: "it's great stuff, the people who consume it are nourished. It's a positive force." Puig is also convinced that film watching is a necessary form of escapism. "They help you to not go crazy. . . . It helped you to hope."[1]

After his studies at the University of Buenos Aires, Puig attempted to establish a career in screenwriting and directing, but the Argentinean film industry proved far too small and saturated to accommodate his ambitions. In 1957, Puig won a scholarship to the Experimental Film Center in Rome.

During the next ten years, he lived and traveled throughout Europe, the United States, and briefly again in South America.

In 1963 while living in New York, Puig began to write his first novel. *Betrayed by Rita Hayworth* was finally published five years later. His second novel, *Heartbreak Tango,* turned out to be popular and drew readers to the earlier work. In 1973, Argentinean censors confiscated all copies of Puig's third book, *The Buenos Aires Affair,* for its portrayal of a sadomasochistic relationship.

In addition to novels, Puig has also written screenplays, two of which, his own adaptations of *Heartbreak Tango* and *Hell Has No Limits,* have won prizes at the San Sebastian Film Festival.

Puig wrote *Kiss of the Spider Woman* in 1976 (published in the United States in 1979), his most successful novel to date. In this book, Puig perfected his cinematic style of writing while exploring his favorite issues: sexual ambiguity and the effects of popular culture on the individual imagination. Puig had already expanded his audience with this book by the time Hector Babenco's Oscar-winning film version jammed movie theaters in 1985. While the film was commercially successful, it misrepresented the book to some extent. The dynamics of the drama and the dimensions of the characters of the book were lost in its translation into film. The film, however, served to expose Puig to the attention of many who might never have read his works.

Puig is the author of three other novels to date, *Pubis Angelical, Eternal Curse on the Reader of These Pages,* and *The Blood of Requited Love.* His books have been published in at least eleven languages, and his importance as an international literary figure continues to grow.

Writing, shooting, and editing—the three main stages in making a film—did not originate simultaneously. At the turn of the century, shooting was the sole stage in making a film. By the 1920s, with the trend having been set by Edwin S. Porter and D.W. Griffith and then reinforced by Sergey Eisenstein, editing became the most essential stage in filmmaking. For a long time, the writing stage was often ignored. Although some artistically accomplished scripts began to appear in the 1920s, it was not until a decade later that the importance of writing was fully understood.

Today, because the techniques and aesthetics of shooting and editing have become highly developed, the success of cinema depends largely upon the writer, upon the inventive ideas and humanistic depth of a film's dramatic content. From a semitechnical genre, as scripts were in the early stages of film history, they have become a fully developed, self-contained, sophisticated literary form, so much so that now screenwriting style even influences contemporary literature. Manuel Puig's novel *Kiss of the Spider Woman* is a quintessential example of such writing, and a familiarity with this text can help the beginning screenwriter learn how to describe scenes and build dialogue; it also serves as a good exercise in translating words into visual images.

Synopsis

In a South American prison, Molina, a window dresser convicted of corrupting minors, retells movies he has seen to his cellmate, Valentin, an intellectual political extremist. They both want to forget about "this filthy cell, and all the rest."[2] The movies are sentimental, sometimes suspenseful, and full of melodramatic clichés.

"She is not a woman like all others," begins Molina, recalling a movie about young, attractive Irena, whose instincts are more like a panther's than a human's. Irena marries an architect but avoids intimacy with him. Meanwhile, the architect's female assistant falls in love with him. Literally turning into a panther, Irena stalks her rival, who manages to get away. In despair, Irena (a woman again) gives herself to her psychiatrist then attacks and kills him. She goes to the zoo and sets a male panther free. Escaping from the cage, the animal knocks her down. When the architect and his assistant arrive, they find Irena dead. They "walk off together arm in arm, trying to forget the terrible spectacle."

Valentin is listening to Molina with interest, even though he considers movies to be "such trivia." He says that he has more important things to think about—the political struggle, social revolution, Marxism. In contrast, Molina, a sentimental, romantic homosexual, is devoid of political interests.

In the next film that Molina relates to Valentin, the action takes place in Paris during World War II. A high-ranking Nazi officer falls in love with a singer, Leni. They are happy together. The Maquis (French underground resistance) contact Leni—they want her to spy for them. She refuses. The head of the group, nicknamed Clubfoot, takes Leni's cousin as a hostage and gives Leni an ultimatum: if she does not help them, they will kill the boy. Leni gets the information. She risks her life and is torn between the patriotism that has awakened within her and her love for the Nazi. Leni is captured by a gang of criminals connected to Clubfoot. She stabs the leader but is shot by one of his men. Leni dies in the arms of her beloved Nazi, who comes too late to rescue her.

Molina tells Valentin about his unhappy love for a waiter, an intelligent, straight man with a family, who would never be his lover. Molina also admits that he does not "feel like" a man and considers himself a woman.

Valentin accuses Molina of being apolitical and of not even knowing who the Maquis were — they were so falsely portrayed in the movie. Offended, Molina replies that feelings, not politics, are important to him.

After eating prison food that was deliberately poisoned, Valentin gets sick. To distract him from his agonies, Molina narrates another movie. It takes place in France in the 1960s and is about a young South American racecar driver from a wealthy family. His father encourages his passion for racing — he wants to keep his son away from the political activities of leftist students. The young man is sensitive to social injustice and tries to be independent of his father's wealth. He meets a successful older Frenchwoman and falls in love with her. But he has to leave her to go back to his own country: his father has been kidnapped by leftist guerrillas. The racer convinces them that he shares their political views and wants to join in their struggle. The guerrillas agree to let his father go in exchange for a large ransom, but at the last moment, they kill the multimillionaire. The young man's lover comes to support him in his grief. Finally, the young man decides "to remain there with the guerrillas, and the woman goes back all alone to her job in Paris, and the parting is really sad, because the two of them actually love one another, but each one belongs to a different world."

Meanwhile, Valentin is in terrible stomach pain. As if in continuation of the movie's story, Molina asks his cellmate about his family. He finds out that Valentin's mother is a wealthy upper-class woman, separated from Valentin's father, who has died recently. Valentin says he does not want his mother to know anything about him or to visit him or to bring him food as Molina's loving mother does.

Valentin continues to suffer from pain and diarrhea. Molina takes care of him devotedly, and Valentin becomes appreciative. To show how much he trusts Molina, he tells him about the codes he uses in his letters to his girlfriend, Marta.

In the prison office, the warden interrogates Molina. The warden tells Molina about a chance of pardon if he provides evidence against his cellmate. The warden reminds Molina about his lonely, ailing mother. Molina persuades the warden to let Valentin recover. Molina asks for some food to be brought in from the outside so that he can tell his cellmate that his, Molina's, mother had visited and brought it. Later, Molina happily takes two large parcels back to the cell and feeds the starving Valentin some choice delicacies.

Torn by the dilemma he faces, tortured by his fears and his love for Valentin, Molina recalls another movie—about a young girl from New York who takes a steamer to go to her husband "whom she's married . . . after only knowing [him] a few days." He is a widower and lives on his own island in the Caribbean. The captain of the steamer feels sorry for the girl because she has no idea what she is getting herself into, but he does not say anything to her. The husband is happy to see her, but everything on the is-land is eerie and frightening—drums in the jungle, shadows and sounds in the mansion, sinister looks by her husband's majordomo, and her husband's first wife's ghost, who haunts the girl. She is confused and afraid. She eventually discovers that the island is in-habited by zombies, the living dead, who work on her husband's plantations and beat the drums at night, and that the majordomo is a witch doctor, who transforms people into zombies. He destroyed her husband's first wife, and now he wants to do the same to her. With his magic, the majordomo makes the ghost of the dead first wife kill the husband, but then he himself is struck dead by light-ning. The girl gives her possessions to the poor and races off to the steamer. "Luckily, it's the same handsome captain who deliv-ered her to the island in the first place . . . the captain tells her not to be afraid, all that's left behind now."

Molina comforts the weak and dizzy Valentin. He washes and feeds him.

In the prison office, the warden asks Molina for any news. "Not too much to tell, I'm afraid," Molina says apologetically. The warden tells Molina that, if there is no news, his cellmate will be "interrogated again, and thoroughly." "Give me just another week, and I'm sure I'll have some information for you," replies Molina. The warden reminds him about the pardon and tells him that he will be transferred to a different cell.

Molina returns to the cell with more food. He admits to Valen-tin that he wants his friendship, even his affection. He also says that, in a week, he will be moved to another cell. Valentin is so upset by this news that he cannot continue his studies. He wants to give Molina the names of his comrades so Molina can contact them if he is let out of jail. "Never, never tell me anything about your comrades," begs Molina. Valentin tries to convince him that he must join a political group when he leaves the prison. "I don't understand any of those things, and I don't believe in them very much either," says Molina. They are both distressed by their expected separation. Their conversation, Molina's tears, and Valentin's attempts to comfort him develop into a love scene.

In the morning, they discuss their relationship. Molina says that he has not been this happy since childhood. Valentin asks him to recount another film, Molina's favorite.

"It takes place in Mexico," starts Molina. "At a masquerade ball, a man and a woman dance together the whole night without revealing their faces." In the morning, the woman disappears without telling him her name. The man, a reporter, cannot forget her. He accidentally comes across a gossipy article in the office about an actress and her "powerful tycoon" lover, which is ready to be published. He recognizes the unusual-looking ring of his mysterious dancing partner in the article's accompanying photograph. He destroys the article, finds the woman, and tells her about his feelings for her. She is attracted to him also, but she is afraid of her powerful lover. The reporter loses his job when the newspaper learns that he destroyed the article. He becomes a vagabond; he "wanders around from bar to bar," works as a laborer, drinks, and writes song lyrics about his love. His health deteriorates, and some time later, the actress finds him in a hospital. She has left her previous lover, so the reporter and she start living together. To support him and to pay off his hospital bills, she becomes a prostitute. When he discovers that she has become a prostitute, he leaves her. She eventually finds him in a shelter for the destitute, but he is dying. On her way back to the place where they lived together, she hears fishermen singing. She recognizes the song. The words were written for her by her unfortunate lover.

In the warden's office, Molina admits that he has no information. "I did everything I could, sir." The warden tells an astonished Molina that he will be let go the next morning anyway.

In the cell, Valentin tells Molina that he wants him to go away happy and to "have good memories of me, like I have of you." Molina resolves to take a message to Valentin's comrades.

According to a police report, several days after his release, Molina called Valentin's comrades from a street phone and asked for a meeting. Molina was followed to the meeting place by police agents. He did not suspect anything. Valentin's comrades, passing by in their car, recognized the agents and fired several shots at Molina. They killed him rather than risk the possibility of his confessing to the police.

In the prison hospital, a doctor administers morphine to Valentin, who is covered with bruises and burns. "A little pinch, and now you'll start feeling less pain." In a drug-induced dream, where images of reality and Molina's films are interwoven and transformed, he sees his girlfriend, Marta. He tells her how much he loves her, asks her for forgiveness, and asks her if the newspaper story, which told of his cellmate's death in a shoot-out, is true. "Let's hope . . . he may have died happily," says Valentin because Molina died like some heroine in the movies he loved to retell.

Like a film script, this novel consists of two types of literary text: dialogue and action description. There are no author digressions, such as those that usually intersperse a novel's text. Puig's main concern is with what people do and say.

Everything that goes on in the cell is expressed through dialogue. The reader finds no descriptions of the cell or of the cellmates, nothing about their facial expressions or gestures. The reader only "hears" what they say. Puig does not even indicate on the written page who says what:

—You were crying out in your sleep.
—Really?
—Yes, you woke me up.
—Sorry.
—How do you feel?

As in good scripts, Puig's dialogue is clearly individualized. Most of the time, the reader recognizes immediately Valentin's abrupt, dry speech: "Look, remember what I told you, no erotic descriptions. This isn't the place for it"; and the soft, imaginative manner of Molina: "It helps me pass the time, watching the shadows when the stove's lit."

The cellmates' dialogue moves the plot forward. Only through the dialogue does the reader come to realize what they are doing:

—If you wash yourself in that freezing shower it certainly will kill you, as sick as you are right now.
—But what is to be done? For the last time, tell me, goddamn it.
—Well, I could help you clean yourself. Look we can heat some water in the pot, we already have two towels, so one we soap up with and you wash the front of yourself, I can do the back for you, and with the other towel slightly wet we sponge off the soap.
—And then my body wouldn't itch so much?

And not by description but by dialogue does the reader learn about Molina's and Valentin's past and about each man's family:

> —Know something? If you didn't tell your mom that she can actually bring food to you each week . . . then you're a fool.
> —I don't want her to feel obligated. I'm here because I asked for it, and she's got nothing to do with it.
> —My mother doesn't come because she's sick, you know?
> —No, you didn't tell me.
> —They told her she can't get out of bed for anything, on account of her heart.

In the beginning of the novel, Valentin talks mostly about facts, Molina about feelings and impressions. "My life is dedicated to political struggle, or, you know, political action . . . there is a purpose behind it, social revolution," says Valentin to Molina, who insists that one should "live for the moment." Gradually, though, their speech patterns change, and Molina speaks more directly and Valentin more emotionally: " 'Never!' What an awful word. Until now I had no idea . . . how awful . . . that word . . . could . . . I'm sorry."

Molina's recollections of the movies are pure description of action, and the dialogue of the movies' characters is given only as reported speech. That is, they are given as indirect quotes, for example: "He asks her what she's trying to forget, and she suggests that he tells her first, then she'll do the same."

Molina inserts into the narration his own remarks and commentaries about the movies' events and characters. Sometimes Valentin makes comments or they discuss it.

> —And the camera again shows you the silvery garden, and there you are in the movies but it's more as if you were a bird taking off because now you see the garden from above, smaller and smaller. . . . Do you like the picture?
> —I don't know yet. And you, why do you like it so much? . . . It's a piece of Nazi junk, or don't you realize?

In contrast to Molina, Puig does not openly provide personal commentaries about the cellmates or the films. Like a screenwriter, he remains "invisible," and the reader learns about his opinions not from the words but from the structure of the novel.

When reading the novel, one strongly senses the presence of a camera. Many of the descriptions, it seems, are made as though through a lens. The imaginary camera tilts up and down, pans, moves in tightly on an object or figure, then recedes to capture the entire scene; sometimes it travels slowly, sometimes quickly: "She looks fairly young . . . petite face, a little catlike, small turned up nose. . . . She looks at her subject: the black panther at the zoo, which was quiet at first, stretched out in its cage. . . . the panther spotted her and began pacing back and forth in its cage and to growl at the girl. . . . It's winter, it's freezing. The trees are bare in the park. There's a cold wind blowing."

Because of his cinematic experience Puig has mastered this literary style, a style in which every sentence "asks" to be incarnated into a visual image in the way a musical score asks to be incarnated into sound. Along with this ability to "see" every word—a typical trait of professional screenwriters—Puig has a specific cinematic sensitivity, which is manifested in his freehanded treatment of time and space in narration. With constant changes from one place to another and from the present to the past, Puig has completely absorbed the dynamic quality of screenwriting.

The tension between the two main "textures"—the prison cell and Molina's movies (that is, the dialogue and the visual descriptions)—determines the plot of the novel. Scenes from Molina's films are interwoven with scenes of the two prisoners' daily lives, their dreams, their growing closeness, friendship, love affair, and parting. The dramatic crosscutting of the textures reinforces each of them. In comparison to the dreariness of the cell, the triviality of the movies appears to be something more meaningful; the constant presence of the films adds a romantic dimension to the relationship of the two cellmates.

Puig uses intercutting from one texture to another as a device to create suspense for the novel's two characters and for the reader. From time to time, for example, Molina stops in the middle of recounting one of his films to coax Valentin into becoming more involved, more intrigued, and more speculative about them: "I like to leave you hanging, that way you enjoy the film more," says Molina. Puig, in turn, interrupts scenes of his characters' lives with Molina's narration of films. By doing so, he keeps the reader in suspense because, most of the time, the reader cares more about the dynamics of the cellmates' relationship than about the films' melodramas.

In the beginning of the novel, there is an enormous contrast between the exotic panther-woman story and the reality of the prison cell, although on a deep, subconscious level the panther-woman is Molina's image of himself: "She's not a woman like all others." The subsequent films that are recounted introduce several other themes, which are repeated over and over again—love at all costs, betrayal, fear, repression, liberation, and sacrifice. Although full of melodramatic clichés, these films create a common ground for two very different individuals. While Molina and Valentin talk about the films, they gradually reveal themselves. The films and the cellmates' lives move closer and closer together, and at the end of the novel, reality and illusion merge. The teller of the films himself becomes a "heroine," and his own life turns out to be no less romantic and unusual than the lives portrayed in his films.

In the last of Molina's recounted films, the heroine becomes a prostitute—she needs money to feed her mortally ill lover. Molina, like the film heroine, continues to collaborate with his jailers to get food for Valentin. In this highly sentimental film, the man dies—as is going to happen to Molina soon—and only his song for his woman is left: "I never thought . . . I could become . . . so obsessed with you. . . . I love you more . . . cry for me." This love confession becomes Valentin's and Molina's, too. After Molina's death, Valentin is "obsessed with" Molina's image, though he has "never thought" he "could become" so.

The films recounted by Molina influence each man's personality: Valentin becomes more human, Molina almost heroic. And they help both men transcend the reality of their predicament. For them, the films are literally a substitute for their lives. This escapism is a matter of survival. The end of every film is experienced by the cellmates as a loss, almost a death. "I've become attached to the characters. And now it's almost over, and it's just like they died," says Valentin.

Just as screenwriters do in developing their scripts, Puig uses the whole range of "cuts" when he switches between textures. He links scenes of the films and of the prison cell for the sake of plot continuity. The cuts move the plot of the novel toward its culmination—Molina's death for Valentin's cause—and toward the resolution, which occurs in Valentin's final enlightening dream, when he comes to accept life the way it is: full of emotions and sentiments, intense, illusive, like Molina's movies.

The substance of this dream and that of the recounted films is almost the same: free flights of fantasy in space; instant transitions forward and backward in time; easy switches of the imagination from the long shot of an entire scene to a close-up of a detail; natural combinations of reality and symbols. Molina's film images are often loosely connected in free associations like the images that fill Valentin's last dream:

I keep swimming underwater . . . it's so very deep . . . the only one who knows for sure is him, if he was sad or happy to die that way, sacrificing himself for a just cause. I think he let himself be killed because that way he could die like some heroine in a movie.

. . . I'm swimming with my head above water now so that way I won't lose sight of the island coast. . . . such a strange woman, with a long dress on, that's shining . . . she's wearing a mask, it's also silver, but . . . poor creature . . . she can't move, there in the deepest part of the jungle she's trapped in a spider's web, or no, the spiderweb is growing out of her own body, she's smiling but a tear rolls out from beneath the mask . . . and I ask her why she's crying and in a close-up that covers the whole screen at the end of the film she answers me that that's just what can never be known, because the ending is enigmatic . . . and the spider woman pointed out to me the way through the forest with her finger, and so I don't know where to even begin to eat so many things I've found now . . . thanks to the spider woman, and after I have one more spoonful of the guavapaste.

Puig makes some cuts by association to bring the textures closer to each other. He switches from the coolness of the dawn that wakes up the panther-woman to the prison cell: "The cold wakes her up, just like us," says Valentin; from a film heroine scared to death somewhere in the jungle to Molina "scared of everything, scared of kidding myself about getting out of here"; from the cellmates' recollections of their last night of intimacy to the Mexican reporter dreaming of his actress with whom he spent just "one night of carnival and that's that."

In the novel, there are also examples of discontinuity "editing," that is, neighboring episodes are sharply mismatched. For instance, a scene in a "dreamy villa in Monte Carlo" is "edited" together with a scene of Valentin suffering from diarrhea. This jump heightens the novel's dramatic expressiveness as such jumps often do in scripts and films.

Some of Puig's cuts are reminiscent of the principle of intellectual montage. By colliding different textures (the reality of the cell; Molina's films; dreams; memories), Puig expresses abstract ideas that are not present in any of the textures individually. They become apparent only when the textures are brought together in sharp juxtaposition. For example, when Puig "edits" together Molina's recollections about his love for a waiter, scenes from a film about a romantic French singer, and scenes of Molina's and Valentin's growing intimacy, Puig's submessage for his cinematic novel becomes clear: that life, films, and dreams have striking similarities; that they influence each other; that film has enormous impact on our existence; that movies are part of our lives; and that it is largely due to them that our sense of reality, like Molina's and Valentin's, "isn't restricted by this cell we live in."

Appendixes
Notes
Index

Appendix A: Exercises

Chapter 1

1. Read the *Nosferatu* script and view the film. Select several scenes from the film and write a description of each. Next, compare your version to the script, paying close attention to the condensed style of the screenplay. Is your version written as concisely? Does it capture the mood of the scenes? Does it describe the action clearly?

2. In two or three sentences, write a brief summary of the *Nosferatu* script, starting with, "A young man, Jonathan Harker, makes a business trip to Count Dracula, who turns out to be a vampire."

3. Write a similar summary for each of several other films that you know well.

Chapter 2

1. Choose your favorite film, watch it several times, then break it down into sequences. Describe each sequence in two or three lines. Notice how they are related to each other. Where and how are parallel actions suggested? Where are the sharpest contrasts between the sequences? Where do the largest and the smallest jumps in time occur and why?

2. Choose a sequence from the same film and break it down into scenes. Examine how they are related to each other.

Chapter 3

1. Using the same film as in the previous exercise, try to define the triangle of plot (opening, climax, and resolution). Which crisis in the film

leads to the climax? What is the main conflict in the film? How active is the opening? What, in the action or in the dialogue, reveals elements of the backstory (that which happened *before* the film began)?

2.   Now it is time to begin your own project—a screenplay for a short dramatic film. Find your subject by developing several premises or by trying several "what if" situations. For example, what if an ordinary clerk is mistaken for an international spy? What if an old cleaning woman is invited to star in a film? What if a schoolgirl, under a spell, is transformed into an adult, yet remains a girl at heart? Find the most workable "what if" for your script, and imagine all of the possibilities inherent in this situation. Remember to keep yourself open and to try different approaches at turning your premise into a story.

Chapter 4

1.   Prepare a written analysis of any main character of the kind presented in chapter 4 for Michael from *The Godfather*. Focus on the stages of the character's development and on the turning point in the character's story. What are the character's goals? Compare the character in the beginning of the film to the same character in the last scene. How has that character changed? (You can do this exercise with Zampano, from *La Strada,* or the protagonist from the film you worked with in the exercises for chapters 2 and 3.)

2.   Write a paragraph about your chosen character's childhood. Also, describe one or two important events in the character's backstory.

3.   In your own script project, identify the protagonist of the story. Describe his or her appearance in detail.

4.   Now write the protagonist's biography (two to three pages), describing his or her childhood and family, the most important events of the protagonist's life, the protagonist's tastes, friends, and occupation. Try to imagine your character in a moment of danger and in a moment of happiness.

Chapter 5

1.   Invent two or three situations of your own with a "hidden bomb"

and a "ticking clock." Now imagine that your audience does not know about the "bomb." Notice how the suspense suddenly disappears.

2. How have you built the dramatic tension in your own script project? At which points do the surprises occur? Do you have a "hidden bomb" in your story? What stands for the "ticking clock?"

Chapter 6

1. For classroom discussion only, the teacher will assign a short story for adaptation. When reading the story, define the scenes that are appropriate for a film script. Omit superfluous scenes and characters. Add scenes that you might find lacking. As in the discussion of *Rashomon*, define the different textures (locations in the story). Make a diagram showing how you plan to switch from one texture to another. Change the time sequence of the story. Try starting the film from the end of the story or from the middle.

2. Working on your individual script project, describe concisely on index cards the scenes of your story that are clear to you at this point. Each scene should be written on a different card. Lay the cards out on a table and find out which scenes are missing. You should work with these index cards throughout the screenwriting process to keep the relationships between the scenes flexible.

Chapter 7

1. For in-class exercise only, analyze the recurring motifs in the scripts discussed in this book. For example, analyze the repetition of Zampano's performance in *La Strada* or the repetition of the same murder in *Rashomon*. What kind of commentary does each author make on the action? Bring in examples of motifs from other films.

2. The class should view several scenes of a film chosen by the teacher, concentrating on close-ups. Then, discuss the function of the close-ups (i.e., whether they are used to establish intimacy with the characters or to single out details necessary to the plot).

3. For your own script project, lay out the index cards containing your scenes. Move the cards around, exchanging the beginning of the

story with the end. Do the same with other scenes. Eliminate unnecessary episodes. When the cards are in a satisfactory order, write a treatment— three and one-half to five pages describing the action in short, concise sentences. Here is an example.

> Central Park, New York. Dawn. Hugh Morgan, a handsome "yuppie," in a tuxedo, is asleep on a bench beneath a tree. A squirrel scrambles up the tree, and a large pinecone falls and hits Hugh on the head. He instantly sits up and, still half asleep, feels for his slippers with his feet. Unable to locate them, he opens his eyes and with astonishment notices that he is wearing his patent leather shoes.
> In the stylish living room of an expensive Chicago co-op, Sue Morgan is talking on the telephone. She is in tears. She tells the police that her husband has disappeared. Yesterday they had celebrated his thirty-third birthday; when all the guests had left, she realized that Hugh was gone, too. She believes he has been kidnapped, although she has no idea who would have done it.

Notice that the treatment is written in the present tense and that every description translates easily into visual images. Note how the action switches from one location to another simply by beginning a new paragraph. Notice also that there is no dialogue. Rarely can a line or two of dialogue be used in a treatment and only when it is absolutely necessary for the description of the action.

Chapter 8

1. Select two or three pages from any script and analyze the function of every line of dialogue. Which lines provide information about the characters? Which ones move the plot forward? Which ones reveal the backstory?

2. Conduct a small survey by asking ten people the same question, for example: How do you feel about Thanksgiving? Make sure that the people you question vary in age, profession, and background. Take notes on the style of their speech and their specific expressions. Notice how their speech works together with their facial expressions, gestures, and body movements. Also notice how these gestures sometimes replace words entirely.

3.   For your script project, try to imagine the way your characters speak and how they would answer the same survey question. Identify the social group to which your characters belong. Is your protagonist a waiter? A member of a rock band? Familiarize yourself with the argot of this group.

Chapter 9

1.   Reread your treatment. Be your own critic—cut as much as you can. Think about your screen story. Eliminate unnecessary episodes and details. Now you are ready to begin writing your screenplay. Do not forget that every scene must have its own headings, in capital letters, indicating whether it is exterior (EXT) or interior (INT), the location, (a park, a street in Paris), and the time (dawn, morning, afternoon, night). In screenplays for short dramatic films, one usually deals with scenes, not with sequences, because often the whole film amounts to just one sequence. When writing a scene, use some of the descriptive material from your treatment, but make it even more concise. You may add some details if needed. In describing characters, do not go into too much detail, do not mention obvious things. The following is an example, using the treatment from the chapter 7 exercise.[1]

EXT. CENTRAL PARK, NEW YORK—DAWN

HUGH MORGAN, a handsome "yuppie," in a tuxedo, is sleeping on a bench beneath a tree. A pinecone falls on his head. He instantly sits up, feels for his slippers with his feet, does not find them, and with astonishment notices his patent leather shoes.

INT. THE MORGANS' LIVING ROOM IN CHICAGO—MORNING

In an expensively stylish living room, pretty SUE MORGAN talks on the phone.

SUE
(in tears)

Last . . . night . . . this birthday party . . . Disappeared.
What? Thirty-three. . . . I am telling you, officer . . .

A CLEANING WOMAN with a vacuum cleaner opens the living room door.

CLEANING WOMAN

Madam, may I . . .

Shaking, SUE motions her away.

SUE

When the guests left, he was gone.
Officer, do something.

A cat jumps in SUE's lap, but she pushes it off.

SUE (continued)

Kidnapped, maybe?!

2.   After you have written the dialogue, try replacing some of the
lines with action.

3.   While writing your screenplay, continue to read a variety of other
scripts and analyze them. How are the scenes organized? How do the
action and the characters develop? How are the pages laid out?

The following page of script is from the screenplay *Moscow on the
Hudson* (screenplay by Paul Mazursky and Leon Capetanos; directed by
Paul Mazursky, 1984).

EXT. EAST SIDE LOWER MANHATTAN—DAY

Passengers getting on a bus.

INT. BUS—DAY

Bus begins to go uptown. Middle-aged FRENCH WOMAN, looking
lost, comes up the aisle and finds a seat next to a Man of about
thirty. Man holds a saxophone case in his lap and is dressed like
any other youngish American. After a moment, the Woman speaks.

FRENCH WOMAN
(accent)

Excuse me, please, sir, Does zis
bus go to ze Lincoln Centaire?

The Man, who is VLADIMIR IVANOFF, speaks with a slight Russian
accent.

VLADIMIR

Did you say Lincoln Center?

FRENCH WOMAN

Oui . . . Yes.

VLADIMIR

Okay, lady. You are on wrong bus.
But it's okay. You can get right
bus. You have to change at 59th
Street for number twenty-two bus.

Is okay, lady. When is time I
tell you and you change. You
get free transfer.

FRENCH WOMAN

Merci . . . Thank you.

VLADIMIR

Sure thing. . . . It's tough to find
way around at first.

They smile at each other.

Appendix B:
Script Sources

Bicycle Thieves by Vittorio De Sica and Cesare Zavattini. London: Lorrimer Publishing, Ltd., 1968.

The Godfather by Mario Puzo and Francis Ford Coppola. Hollywood: Script City, n.d.

Nosferatu, a Symphony of Horror by Henrik Galeen, in *Masterworks of the German Cinema*. New York: Harper & Row, 1973.

Notorious by Ben Hecht and Alfred Hitchcock. Hollywood: Script City, n.d.

Rashomon by Akira Kurosawa and Shinobu Hashimoto, in *Rashomon*, Donald Richie, ed. New Brunswick: Rutgers University Press, 1987.

The Servant by Harold Pinter, in *Five Screenplays*, by Harold Pinter. New York: Grove Press, n.d.

La Strada by Federico Fellini, Tullio Pinelli, with Ennio Flaiano, in *La Strada*, Peter Bondanella and Manuela Gieri, eds. New Brunswick: Rutgers University Press, 1987.

Viridiana by Luis Buñuel and Julio Alejandro, in *Three Screenplays*, by Luis Buñuel. New York: Orion Press, 1969.

All of the films discussed in this book can be rented or purchased as video cassettes as can the film version of *Kiss of the Spider Woman*. Scripts from Script City can be purchased by mail only, at the following address:

Script City
1765 North Highland
#760AF
Hollywood, CA 90028

Notes

1.
The Beginning of Screenwriting

1. Lewis Jacobs, *The Rise of the American Film*. New York: Harcourt, Brace & Co., 1939, pp. 27–28.

2. Jacobs, p. 43.

3. Jacobs, p. 44.

4. E. F. Barker, *Successful Photo-Play Writing*. New York: Eric Publishing Co., 1914.

5. Although eventually even the greatest American authors like William Faulkner and Eugene O'Neill would write film scripts, they saw it as something unworthy and base. It is known, for example, that for the theater, O'Neill chose the more intimate and careful method of writing by hand; for the screen, however, he worked in a more businesslike manner at the typewriter.

6. This and all other quotes of the script in this chapter are from *Nosferatu, a Symphony of Horror,* by Henrik Galeen published in *Masterworks of the German Cinema*. New York: Harper & Row, 1973.

7. The reader of a screenplay has to visualize what is going on, not just read about it, and thus can be called the viewer as well as the reader.

8. The desire to overcome the static nature of subtitles was familiar to every screenwriter of the silent era. In the 1920s, for example, the subtitles in Russian films were broken down into many parts and inserted in these smaller portions to avoid slowing down the tempo of the film. Sometimes the subtitles were simply superimposed over the shots.

2.
Script Composition

1. Angelo Solmi, *Fellini*. London: Merlin Press, 1967, p. 109.

2. Solmi, p. 117.

3. Solmi, p. 116.

4. In *La Strada,* Peter Bondanella and Manuela Gieri, eds. New Brunswick: Rutgers University Press, 1987. This is a so-called cutting continuity, which is done *after* the film has been released and every shot has become stabilized within itself and in relation to the other shots. It contains technical information, but it is entirely different from the screenplay of a novice screenwriter who writes instructions to the camera and actors ("directs on paper"), trespassing upon the territory of the director and the cameraman.

5. A *shot* is a piece of film recorded from the moment the camera starts to the moment it stops. Depending on the size of the image, the shots are defined as long shot (LS), medium shot (MS), close-up (CU), medium close-up (MCU), and extreme close-up (ECU).

6. The original script—*La Strada: Sceneggiatura originale di Federico Fellini e Tullio Pinelli* (Rome: Edizioni Bianco e Nero, 1955)—has never been translated into English in its entirety. The script was abridged in some parts and somewhat altered in the process of shooting the film, but the basic story, the characters, and the organization remained exactly the same.

7. A *scene* is a group of shots related to one another.

8. The original script, *La Strada: Sceneggiatura.*

9. This sequence, for example, consists of three scenes. Each of them differs in location and general mood, but together they form a dramatic unity, a finished piece of action. Scene one: Zampano and Gelsomina perform together in the open air in the daytime with many people around them and much excitement. Scene two: Zampano and Gelsomina are in a restaurant late at night. The intimate atmosphere suddenly changes to Gelsomina's being left alone in the road. Scene three: in the dawn and early morning, Gelsomina sits alone at the side of the road. Her dejection is in sharp contrast to the mood in the restaurant. When someone tells her where Zampano is, her sudden flight there finishes the sequence and establishes a bridge between this sequence and the next.

10. In the process of shooting, Fellini replaced Gelsomina's homesickness in the sea scene with her full acceptance of her new life. Additionally, in the film as compared to the screenplay, several sequences were shortened, and everything that detracted from the main line of the plot was eliminated.

11. It is unusual to accentuate the "seams" between the sequences by bringing the headings into a script. But making films in a fragmentary style is Fellini's trademark; even the organization of his scripts reveals this method.

3.
Opening, Climax, Resolution

1. All quotes of the screenplay in this chapter are from Harold Pinter, *The Servant,* published in Harold Pinter, *Five Screenplays.* New York: Grove Press, n.d.

2. The *backstory* is a screenwriter's term for the life of the film's characters prior to the beginning of the film. Although this term is not encountered in critical or scholarly literature, it is useful in the film industry and in the study of screenwriting.

4.
Character Development

1. All quotes of the screenplay are from Mario Puzo and Francis Ford Coppola, *The Godfather*. Hollywood: Script City, n.d.
2. The scene was omitted from the film.

5.
The Construction of Suspense

1. François Truffaut, *Hitchcock*. New York: Simon and Schuster, 1966, p. 121.
2. Leonard Leff, *Hitchcock and Selznick: The Rich and Strange Collaboration of Alfred Hitchcock and David O. Selznick*. New York: Weidenfield & Nicolson, 1988, p. 179.
3. Truffaut, p. 121.
4. Truffaut, p. 52.
5. All quotes of the script are from Ben Hecht and Alfred Hitchcock, *Notorious*. Hollywood: Script City, n.d.
6. Truffaut, pp. 121–22.

6.
Transforming Literature into Cinematic Space and Time

1. All of Kurosawa's quotes are from Akira Kurosawa, *Something Like an Autobiography*. New York: Vintage Books, 1983.
2. Richard Griffith, "Review." *Saturday Review*, 19 January 1952, p. 33.
3. *Rashomon* script, in *Rashomon*, Donald Richie, ed. New Brunswick: Rutgers University Press, 1987. Note how this text is functional, yet it has its literary merits — a distinctive rhythm of short, energetic sentences and elegance in its clarity and leanness. It even has a certain gracefulness — "they recede into the distance."
4. Ryūnosuke Akutagawa, "The Rasho Gate," in *Rashomon*, Donald Richie, ed. New Brunswick: Rutgers University Press, 1987. Although in this edition the short story is called "Rashomon," the title "The Rasho Gate" is used in this chapter to avoid confusion.
5. *Rashomon*, script.
6. *Rashomon*, script.
7. Ryūnosuke Akutagawa, "In a Grove," in *Rashomon*, Donald Richie, ed. New Brunswick: Rutgers University Press, 1987.
8. According to Kurosawa, when the shooting took place, "The Rasho gate we built . . . was extraordinarily large for an open set. . . . Because the gate set was so huge, the job of creating rainfall on it was a major operation. We borrowed

fire engines and turned on the studio's hoses to full capacity."

9. For the sake of concentration, the definition of the term *story* is considerably simplified.

7.
Details, Motifs, and the Director's Commentaries

1. Francisco Aranda, *Luis Buñuel: A Critical Biography*. New York: Da Capo Press, 1976, p. 56.

2. Aranda, p. 54.

3. Although several others tried to insert close-ups into their films before D. W. Griffith did (Englishmen G. A. Smith and James Williamson and the American Edwin S. Porter), most of these close-ups were crude. The truly narrative function of the close-up had not been fully realized before Griffith's time. Even the famous medium close-up of a cowboy firing directly at the audience in Porter's *Great Train Robbery* (1903) was actually extraneous to the plot. It was used at the beginning of the film or at the end, according to the exhibitor's taste. Either way, the story of the film was not changed.

4. Luis Buñuel and Julio Alejandro, *Viridiana,* in Luis Buñuel, *Three Screenplays*. New York: Orion Press, 1969.

5. When close-ups first appeared on the screen, most of which focused on the actors' faces, the public would shout, "Show us their feet." When watching *Viridiana,* from time to time the audience is ready to demand to be shown the actors' faces.

8.
Screen Dialogue

1. The film's original title, *Ladri di Biciclette,* translates as *Bicycle Thieves* (corresponding to the main idea of the film that the one whose bicycle is stolen becomes a thief himself), but it is often referred to as *The Bicycle Thief.*

2. Vittorio De Sica, "How I Direct My Films," in Vittorio De Sica, *Miracle in Milan*. New York: Orion Press, 1968, p. 3.

3. De Sica, *Miracle in Milan.*

4. All quotes from the script in this chapter are from Vittorio De Sica and Cesare Zavattini, *Bicycle Thieves*. London: Lorrimer Publishing, Ltd., 1968.

9.
The Screenplay as a Model for Literature

1. Inga Karetnikova and Susanna Barber, "Cinematic Qualities in the Novel *Kiss of the Spider Woman." Film Literature Quarterly,* 1987, 15(3): 165.

2. All quotes in this chapter are from Manuel Puig, *Kiss of the Spider Woman*. New York: Vintage Books, 1980.

Appendix A.
Exercises

1. For a more detailed look at the format of a screenplay, see Michael Hauge, *Writing Screenplays That Sell*. New York: McGraw-Hill, 1988, chapter 6.

Index

Inga Karetnikova, a former Guggenheim, Carnegie-Mellon, and Radcliffe Institute Fellow, has conducted numerous workshops on film and art in many colleges and universities across the United States. Most recently, she was a Visiting Associate Professor of Film at Boston University. Author of *Eisenstein's Mexican Drawings* (Carucci Publishers, Rome), she is presently a consultant and writer for the BBC in London. She lives in Cambridge, Massachusetts.